GW00759316

THE AYLESBURY DUCK

by

James Edward Goodwin

Published by

MELROSE BOOKS

An Imprint of Melrose Press Limited
St Thomas Place, Ely
Cambridgeshire
CB7 4GG, UK
www.melrosebooks.com

FIRST EDITION

Cover designed by Amanda Barrett Creative Design

ISBN 1 905226 62 4

Printed and bound in Great Britain by:
CPI Bath, Lower Bristol Road,
Bath, BA2 3BL, UK

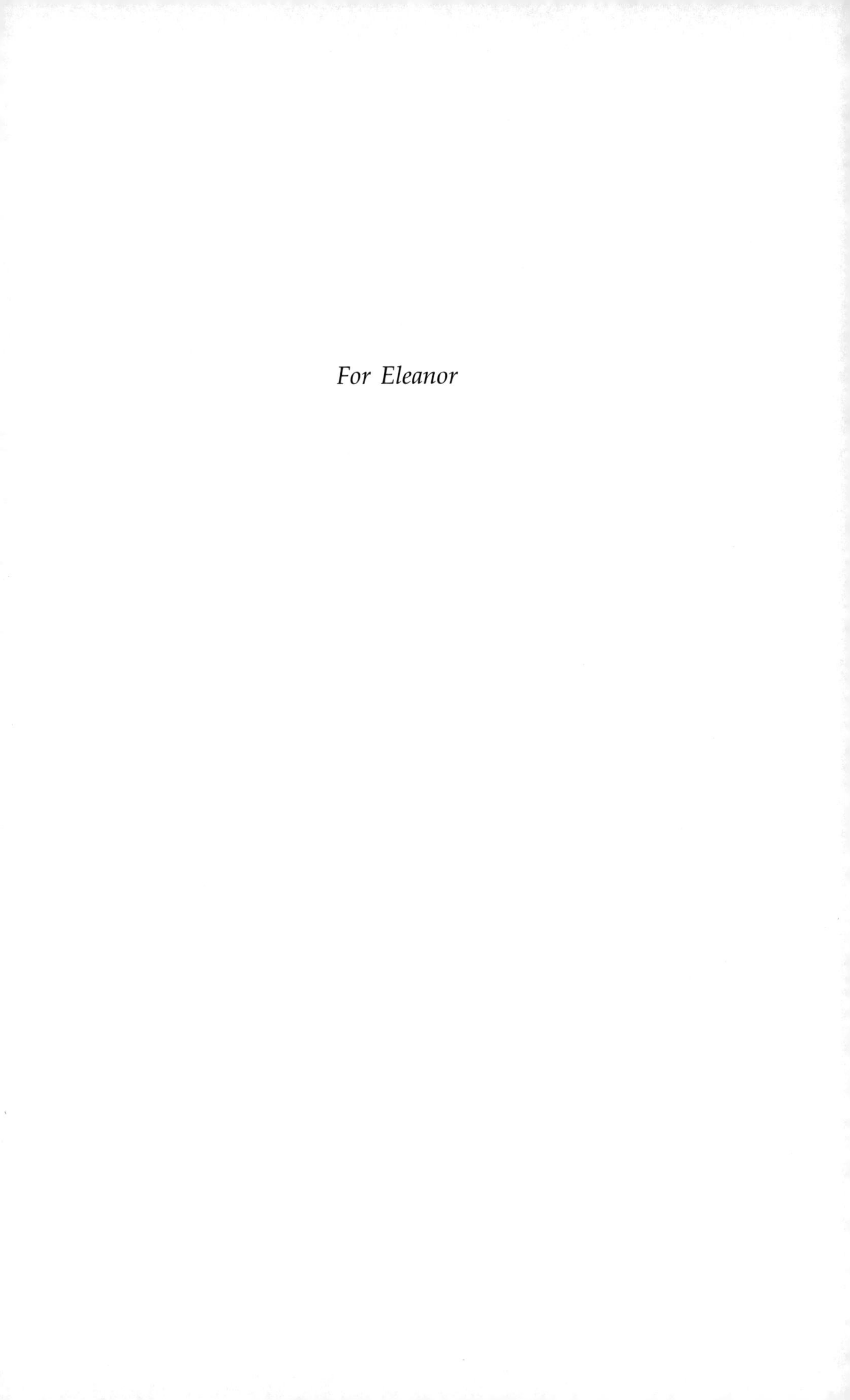

For Eleanor

Acknowledgements

I wish to acknowledge the help and support I have received in the publishing of this book.

To my in-laws Jimmy and Emily Cochrane, to Barbara and Roy Taylor-Dear for Barbara's typing, encouragement and all over help, to Mike Davies for his 'Foreword', and my special thanks are due to my beloved wife Eleanor, without whose patience and advice I would have been lost.

Lastly, but certainly not least, to all those at Melrose Books for their professionalism and guidance. To Jill, Sophie, Bryan Carpenter, Austin, Alan Barker and everyone at Melrose Books I say Thank You.

Foreword

Somewhere in the bowels of New Scotland Yard there is a film of Park Lane taken from the top of Wellington Arch. The year is 1964, and the capital's traffic is practically at a standstill, because this is the time of one of the Commonwealth Conferences. At first glance it would appear that nothing will ever move again in Park Lane, but at the top right of the picture a white dot appears followed immediately by another. These dots resolve themselves into motorcycle helmets and as they move towards the camera the traffic begins to ease, like sheep marshalled by a pair of dogs. In a matter of two minutes the road is clear for a series of black, diplomatic limousines which sweep majestically on their way to St James' Palace, escorted by further motor cyclists. Behind them Park Lane begins to fill up again. Under the first of the white helmets was the author of this book, a professional of his time and, I am proud to say, a friend.

I first came across Jim the Bike when I was charged with the safety of an African potentate whose name and country I have quite forgotten. To help us get about London and to ensure he got to his appointments on time, I was given a two-bike escort, a luxury that was new to me. Jim and his buddy Stan Gannon duly appeared, to be briefed by me. It was not long before I realised that all I had to do was give them a programme of times and places and let them get on with it.

Among the places the potentate visited was the Tower of London, where he was entertained by the Constable. Having eaten, my merry men and I stepped outside to the battlements to look at the tourists round the Green. Jim moved away from us, deftly inserted his helmet under the shoulder of his jacket and proceeded to give us, in ringing tones, the whole of Richard's opening speech from Richard The Third, while capering about the battlements. Our applause was as nothing compared with the cheers from the tourists and Jim took three bows before we left to take our charge home. This seems to me to be the essence of Jim Goodwin. A professional to the fingertips, but a man able to see the funny side of life. A superb raconteur and sharp wit, he is always at the centre of any laughter that is going. His book tells it like it was in those heady days of 60's London, when being a policeman was to be a useful, respected member of the community.

Mike Davies

Prologue

What you're about to read took place over varying times and obviously in ever-changing circumstances.

Some of these stories may fall out of chronological order; they come as I remember them, following tasks I had to undertake.

You will read of my days in the Police Force on the streets of London, in which I served during the 1950s–1970s. I was active in several different divisions; from 'Foot Duty' to 'Traffic Patrol.'

I came in very close contact with many heads of states, and kings and queens.

Some of the stories that you are about to encounter are very dramatic and may be painful to read, while others are very amusing and even a little naughty.

The opinions I express are my own, and nothing more. There may be some moments of conduct about which you may wonder and which I may explain. I had very good personal reasons for the way I took care of certain situations and now have to make up my mind whether to explain them all to you or not, so please bear with me as I take a look back and put the pieces together. I was a young red-blooded and excitable policeman and really enjoyed the job at hand.

Part One

Aylesbury up to my National Service

I was born on the second of March 1930, the son of a newsagent, William Henry Goodwin and my mother Lillian Elizabeth Goodwin (nee Bull). I was born in the early hours of the morning in a small cottage in a com chandler's yard at Britannia Street, in Aylesbury, Buckinghamshire. Already arrived were my brothers William Percival and Ronald Peter.

My first memory was being able to see along the top of the table if I stood on my toes and pulled myself up with my arms. I can also remember that the accumulator for the wireless stood on a cupboard inside the door and could be seen as one stepped down into the only downstairs room in the cottage. Aylesbury always had a lovely comforting smell about the place and I can remember it to this day. The fact that there was an ink works near the iron bridge that crossed the railway line and that the cattle market was held to the rear and to the right of the Town Hall at the bottom of Market Square may have had something to do with it.

Later the family was enlarged by the arrival of brother George Frank and then finally by my sister Rita Elizabeth. I sense that my parents gave up procreating after the safe arrival of Rita.

We then took up residence in a house in Lee Road, Southcourt situated off the Stoke Mandeville road to the south-west of the centre of the town. We then moved across Lee Road to a house almost opposite which had a back garden that faced onto fields, with the nearest village three miles away across them. During any spare time, that is when I was not at school, I spent all of my time across those fields. To get to them I had to climb the garden fence, cross a small stream and there I was in my element. Brother Ron informed me years later, over fifty in fact, that I had what I called a 'nipping pole' for vaulting over the stream. About three fields further on there was Pebble Brook, much wider and needed to be waded across to get to the other side but it was only a few inches deep and could be easily forded. Pebble Brook was a source of nourishment to me, supplying water cress in abundance. All I needed to do was wash off the snails and it satisfied my appetite for the time being. I also found the the leaf buds of the hawthorn hedges quite palatable. I managed to survive the whole of the day in the fields and would come home as the sun just began to set. My mother would often relate to friends that she would see this small creature coming home and casting a large (lengthy) shadow behind him. And that was our Jim coming home.

We had a lot of love in our family and were well cared for. It was years later that I came to realize the terrible strain it must have been to keep five children clothed and fed on a very small income. The food we had was basic but very filling: suet puddings were the order of the day as my father used to say they stick your ribs together. One of these I can remember to this day and that was a suet pudding containing cut up streaky bacon and with the addition of some sage this was boiled in a cloth and combined with boiled potatoes, broad beans and gravy, it was tasty and very filling. Often my parents would give me a penny and off I would go to the baker's shop, which still exists to this day, and buy a pennyworth of stale cakes. You got a baker's dozen for a penny and the fact that they were only a day old meant it was wonderful value. I'd sit on a grass bank across the road from the bakers and consume the lot. I always had a very healthy appetite and when my brothers or my sister left anything on their plate I always cleared it up. The fact that I was so active in my exploration of the fields around meant that I burnt up a lot of energy and never put on any spare fat. In fact, in those days I ate almost as much as my father.

At this time my father would do his paper round in the morning; going as far as Aston Clinton on the Tring Road and Western Turville. He would then come home for his breakfast and off he would go to sell papers in Aylesbury Market Square. Sunday was a special day as Dad would always lay a small bar of Cadbury's on our pillows when he came in for his breakfast. My treat that particular day, and it was the only day of the week when my father had bacon and egg, was a nice thick slice of bread wiped round the frying pan.

In early 1939 we moved to Cranbrook Road, Ilford where we lived above a newsagents and tobacconists, that my father was being trained to run. After about six months we took up permanent residence at Milligans Shop, 23 Darnley Road in Strood in Kent. When war was declared, all the children, that's us, were transferred to relatives in Hertfordshire and Buckinghamshire. Ron, George and I went to my grandparents who lived in Tring. However we seemed to clash with one and another so George and I were transferred to my great aunt Ellen's at Stone, a village three miles to the west of Aylesbury, which we had only left less than a year before. The house, one of a terrace of four Victorian houses overlooked the Vale of Aylesbury and was situated in Eythrope Road. We had great times there coupled with a few miserable moments when we missed being with our parents. To get us out of the house on Sundays we joined the choir at the village Church and so had to attend Matins in the morning, Sunday School in the afternoon and then, to round off the day, Evensong.

We attended the village school where we received a very good grounding, which included digging trenches in the hard sand playground. It was there I took an examination and received a scholarship to Sir Joseph Dilliamson's Mathematical School at Rochester that was just over the Medway from Strood. As I was an evacuee I instead went to the Ealing County School for Boys that had also been evacuated to Aylesbury and occupied part of the Aylesbury Grammar School. After less than a year George and I went back to Strood; the Battle of Britain having been fought and won. At the Math School, lessons were often interrupted by air raid warnings as we were under the flight path to London and quite close to Chatham Dockyard.

However I managed to get my School Certificate although the mish-mash of subjects I passed in left something to be desired. I stayed on at school until I was conscripted into the Army. I was sent to Catterick where, after basic training, I was trained as a Telegraphic Mechanic, my Regiment being the Royal Corps of Signals, and then finally trained as a Cipher Mechanic and then off to the Middle East Cipher School at El Ballah in the Suez Canal zone in Egypt.

Demobbed I took up employment in the City of London as a clerk to a small family company at Crutched Friars, where lunch was taken in the local eel and pie shop and then I listened to the speakers at Tower Hill before going back to the office. I lasted just the six months' probationary period and left.

This is where the story begins.

Part Two

Metropolitan Police, training at Hendon. Posting to Marylebone Lane in the West End. Characters and Incidents.

I joined the Metropolitan Police on the 19th February 1951 and was trained at Hendon. The school was situated in Aerodrome Road, Colindale. It contained not only the training school for new recruits but also the Driving School and the CID school. I had travelled from Strood by train to Charing Cross and then took the Northern Line to Colindale where, after a five minute walk, I arrived.

We were kitted out with our uniforms and allocated our numerals to be affixed to the same. The next day we got down to the business of being taught. We had to learn from the Instruction Book various and also numerous items. Some were known as 'A' reports which had to be learnt by rote, that is, parrot fashion. Others, 'B' reports, we had to absorb so that we had a good working knowledge of them. Combined with this was the Knowledge and Reasoning which having been set an illustration of an incident one had to work out, in sequence, the way one would deal with it. In other words how we would apply what we had been taught in a practical manner.

At the beginning we would only have one 'A' report to learn by heart and the method I used was to read the whole thing through and then start at the beginning, learning the first sentence by heart and then after reading that sentence through, move onto the next and so on. As I repeated the first sentence followed by the rest it all dropped into place, and even today, half a century later, I can still remember some of them.

One statement that has always stuck in my mind is that, 'Idle and silly remarks are unworthy of notice and should be disregarded'. I sometimes think that it should instilled in people's minds from a very early age: it would go a long way to solving a lot of problems.

In roadways of the school they would set up an accident which we would then have to go through; dealing with anyone who was injured, the driver of the vehicle and complete the accident report book to the satisfaction of the instructors. We all had things out of sequence but gradually towards the end of our training we knew exactly what to do. Although the thought of having to deal with the real thing out on the streets, in front of the general public, was another matter.

One also had to play act: giving evidence in court; addressing the 'magistrate' in the correct manner and being capable of standing to the questioning one was put through. Then came the final examination: various 'A' reports to be written out word perfectly and Knowledge and Reasoning scenarios to be dealt with. I passed and was posted to Marylebone Lane Police Station on 'D' division, situated between Wigmore Street and Oxford Street in the centre of the West End of London.

I was accommodated at Elliott House in Molyneux Street which runs parallel to the Edware Road. It was nice to be so near the centre of things and to walk to the Station would take, at a gentle pace, about fifteen minutes through some of the nicest squares in London.

FOOT DUTY

I was quite prepared for any emergency or to act as a Constable in upholding the law in my own inexperienced way, or to help somebody in distress, but I wasn't ready to help anybody with directions. The feeling as you walk to the police station for the first time not really knowing its exact location, and the fear or feeling of inadequacy if someone were to come up to you to ask the way or make inquiries regarding a bus or whatever, had me at a loss.

I walked to the station with Pete Skelley that morning, your average build of a bloke who was the son of a policeman. He wasn't really the sort of man you would want to socialize with and he seemed like a bit of a bully boy, who although not on the same course as me at Hendon, was also on his way to his new posting.

At the corner of Baker Street and Crawford Street our worst fears were realized when a middle-aged well-spoken couple stopped us. My heart must have skipped a beat. Apparently we must have looked brand new to them, as they wished to explain to us for some reason, that they would never have referred to policemen as 'bobbies,' but gave them their full title as 'Roberts'.

Well it was a nice introduction to the general public which has stayed with me to this very day. The term 'bobby' refers to Sir Robert Peel who was the founder of the Metropolitan Police Force.

Once I arrived at the station, I had to have an interview with the man in charge, a chief inspector who I remember being terrified of, as you were when it came to anyone with rank. Nowadays it's a chief superintendent or even a commander who may be in charge. A quick tour of the station premises to show you where everything was, and then off in the Morris J4 van to Albany Street to be interviewed and welcomed by the man in charge of my division. After that you would be taken back to the section house to change numerals on your epaulettes and to prepare for the real job the following day.

One had to learn the beats, attend court, and know where the witness box was. Then one had to listen to the various cases and to generally get the atmosphere and become familiar with magistrates and to learn how they approached different cases. One was attached to the CID for a week and to the Traffic Patrol for another week. All in all about a month was spent in learning things.

When learning beats I quickly discovered that no one policeman was like another; they all had their idiosyncrasies in the way in which they approached their job.

I found that the pre-war constables had the greatest charisma; they were the real coppers that I knew, feared and respected as a child.

Reg Brinds was a pre-war copper, a lovely man who would be there to guide people like me who had just started on the job. He was a great inspiration to me and gave great encouragement to follow. Then there were the 'Freezer Frosts' and 'Timber Woods'; they were characters and most had been through the blitz. Quite a few had been called up during the war.

It's interesting to note that the Metropolitan Police were called up in batches of 300. Some went off to the Navy, some to the Airborne, some to the Commandos, and the Royal Air Force; all together they stamped their individual style on various arms of the services they went to. A few were commissioned and quite a few bravery awards were collected along the way.

It was at this time that I had come to realize that in London in particular, as a policeman I had a certain sense, not of importance, but of representing all the law-abiding citizens and of being available to help ensure that their lives were as peaceful as possible. People did look up to you and expected that while you were about, all would be well with the world. You always met the characters in the local neighbourhood and would stop to chat with them. One gradually picked up local knowledge: street names, bus routes and the various other essential items that go with the job. I often found that the easiest way to learn was to ask your friendly bobby. There was a fountain of knowledge at the station and there were always those ready to help. Gradually I developed that gait; that style of walking that enabled me to fill eight hours of duty with gentle perambulation.

There was one policeman at Marylebone Lane who years before the war, before he joined the police force, had been a butler and could remember Baker Street when it was private houses. He walked with a style of his own, as I developed mine.

UNIFORM

I was one of the first policemen at my station to arrive wearing a collar and tie, most of the lads were still wearing the tunic buttoned up right to the throat.

On ceremonial occasions we had to wear our dress uniforms that were of this style. They were made of a very heavy moleskin material; both the trousers and the tunic and we would only wear a vest and underpants underneath as they became very hot and sticky. There were no pockets on the outside of the tunic and the waist was held in by a patent leather belt fastened by a serpentine hook, similar in everyway to those on the belts that I had as a young boy. We were also supplied with a cape made of a very strong oilskin material used for dress occasions to be rolled up and hooked to the belt. These same capes, during the winter months, worn over the greatcoat gave us protection against the elements, although after an eight hour tour I was always pleased to take the weight off, as they gradually began to tell as the tour of duty went on. Those capes were eventually replaced by others of a more rubbery texture and then taken out of service all together.

The helmet, when I first joined, had a matt black badge with only the Royal Cipher in chrome, these were also updated. We finished with a complete chrome badge which I always thought cheapened the appearance. We had to wear the issued woollen gloves which I never found to be the most attractive. They kept your hands warm but didn't seem part of me. I wore leather gloves when I could get away with it. One or two of the sergeants would point out that leather gloves were for inspectors and so I should desist wearing them. I wouldn't say anything of course and continued wearing them. They made their point and had done their duty.

I remember being on school crossing duty at Lisson Grove, near Marylebone Railway Station, the most unattractive part of Marylebone Lane's ground. It was during the winter at about 4 p.m., and I remember it being very dark. The wind was blowing and the rain was falling down hard, so in order to protect my neck I'd turned my collar up and carried on with the job at hand, when suddenly a senior officer in a police car pulled over to give me a bollocking for having my collar up. The fact that he had to open the window to do so and the fact that the front of his tunic was covered in fag ash, made a farce of the whole incident and insinuated that he was so proud of the way he looked, was a joke. Sometimes in the force you just had to grit your teeth and count to ten with idiots like him about trying to boost their own ego.

Towards the bottom end of Baker Street is Portman Square with Wigmore Street going off to the east. At its bottom corner going off to the west was Bryanston Street and going out of the north-west corner is Gloucester Place that runs parrallel to Baker Street.

In the Fifties, when I first saw Portman Square there was a bomb site in the north-west corner of Portman Square which had been levelled and was used as a car park. The Churchill Hotel now stands there and on the south of the square the Marylebone Police Station stands and the old one where I had such an enjoyable time has been demolished and is replaced by offices.

Going up the east side of the Square there was and possibly still is, a Christian Science office and outside stood a lectern with glass covering the open pages of the Bible giving the thought for the day. On night duty I would always stop and read this as it passed a few well-meaning minutes for me.

Further up Baker Street on the west side was another bomb site which had been levelled and was used by the various American services as a car park. It had been cleared below pavement level and one looked down into it. Further on and on the same side is the headquarters of Messrs Marks and Spencer and in my early days there existed a pedestrian covered bridge linking the back of Marks and Spencer to the building across the mews. Historically this was of great interest to me as it was in the office building in Baker Street that the Special Operations Executive had their headquarters and agents prepared to go into occupied Europe, after training and briefing, would pass through, leaving behind all their clothing, watches and everything that would give their identity away. They would cross over the footbridge, be kitted out with their new identity and clothing and all the paraphernalia that went with it and then be taken to Elstreet Airfield where they would be flown out to their destinations and an uncertain fate. In 1951 there was a room full of clothing and the personal effects of those that had failed to return. There were so many derelict buildings on Marylebone Lane's ground that it took some considerable time for it to regain its former glory.

On a lighter note on eleven beat at the top end of Baker Street on the north side of Marylebone Road, two blocks to the west of Marylebone Circus, was the Marylebone Bridge Club and if on night duty on this beat one always looked in to see that everything was in order and to enjoy the sandwich and beer that had been provided for their local constable. One entered, quietly nodded acknowledgement to everyone, enjoyed the refreshment and went about one's beat.

At Marylebone Lane there were two people who lived on a couple of our beats that need mentioning. One was a lady who lived in a flat above a shop in Marylebone High Street and would request an officer to attend her. She was well known at the station in as much that her request was a regular and frequent one. In consequence of this the duty sergeant, when sending you off to call on this lady would tell you that when you arrived there you would find a man from the Electricity Board, a man from the Gas Board, a postman and a fireman in plain clothes. When you arrived there they all were drinking cups of tea and eating a few dainty biscuits. You joined this happy throng, thanked the lady for the refreshments and went about your beat.

No one has ever explained why this happened. Possibly she just liked the company of men. There was certainly nothing of a sexual nature about the affair: her conversation was on the current climate, both weather-wise and politically, and she had obvious satisfaction in serving the tea and biscuits to those assembled. You could never be sure what you may have found there when called, however you had to take no chances that the lady was crying wolf when in fact she may have needed police assistance.

The other character was an antique dealer by the name of Mudd who had his business just off the High Street in Devonshire Street. Now, when posted to that beat night duty, the sergeant would warm you of the man you would be confronted with. When you had tried the door to his premises to see that it was secure it would suddenly open and a middle-aged gentleman would invite you in for a whiskey. What you did then, as suggested by the sergeant, was to accept his kind invitation and enter the living accommodation, beautifully furnished as one would expect, but Mr Mudd would guide you through to the bedroom and sit you on the bed explaining that the lounge was overlooked and he didn't want to get you into trouble for drinking on duty. The whole of what was taking place had already been explained to you by the sergeant as if it was a scene from a play. Mr Mudd would reappear with a treble single malt, hand it to you and throw on the bed to one side a packet of twenty cigarettes. These, as instructed by the sergeant you pocketed, sipped the malt slowly and then with a quickening pace, you looked at your watch and said, 'Oh, dear me I have to go as I have to meet the sergeant'. This was completely untrue but was suggested as a way out by the sergeant and you got up and left thanking Mr Mudd for his kind hospitality and went. I am certain that Mr Mudd knew that this was about to happen and the reason for the original invitation was to have the company of a young policeman if only for a few minutes. Perhaps after one had left his imagination ran riot, or perhaps he just sat down and pondered on his loneliness, one just does not know.

QUEEN POINT

One of the most tiresome jobs whilst at Marylebone Lane was having to be on traffic point at Marble Arch. Bearing in mind that it was the only traffic point we had I shouldn't complain. We had to control the traffic coming from Park Lane, Oxford Street, Bayswater Road, Edgware Road and Cumberland Place. Now the secret was this, if Park Lane became snarled up, Piccadilly followed and then Regent Street, back to Marble Arch via Oxford Street. The same would apply in an anti-clockwise direction, so all I had to do was to keep things moving. You stood in the roadway and had the buses just missing you as they swung round Marble Arch. This went on for eight hours less the forty-five minutes you had as a meal break, actually it was slightly longer than that. You had to walk to Marylebone Lane, have the forty-five minute break and then walk back. If it was a miserable day I ambled there and back hoping that the relief on the traffic point was so busy he hadn't realized that I was late back.

I found that to keep myself busy on the point I would deliberately do correct signals as displayed in the Highway Code. It was easy to relax and to give sloppy but adequate signals but it helped the time to pass more quickly if you felt that you were putting some effort into it. On one occasion I noticed that the constables from Hyde Park Station was busy just inside the gates of the park and thought to myself they must be having some sort of purge. I kept the traffic moving, whilst holding up the traffic that had come from Marble Arch, Bayswater and Edgware Road. When I thought it was fair to let the other traffic move, I held up my right arm and stopped the Park Lane traffic. When it had stopped I then turned ninety degrees to see to the stationary traffic, only to realize the green Lagonda I had been holding up for all of three minutes contained people I instantly recognized:, Her Majesty the Queen sitting next to HRH Prince Philip, who was driving the car with its roof down. They were on their way from Windsor to Buckingham Palace and they were both laughing so I don't think they were too displeased. Their presence made me understand all the activity in the park. It would have been nice if I had been informed that they were on their way.

I telephoned the superintendent at Hyde Park Police Station to let him know what had happened and to tell him that I would have appreciated some prior information. He seemed quite disturbed about the incident but I explained that they were both laughing after my salute, waving them on and a mouthed 'sorry'.

When it rained there was a large original white rubber coat to wear. This was stored in Marble Arch itself but it was so heavy that it was a job to lift your arms when you had it on. Except in a real downpour the coat remained on its hook out of the way.

If you wanted to go for a pee you would have to leave your point and go into the Arch, have a quick cigarette and then head back out to sort the chaos that the traffic had got itself into. This was the most enjoyable part of the job, full of activity and verbal abuse between the car drivers and the bus drivers. Calm was soon restored and the direction of traffic continued until the end of your tour of duty. Your arms did ache but after a few days of it you became fitter and the muscles that you had seldom used in your life before ceased to be a problem.

THE MARBLE ARCH KNOB

Marble Arch itself is a fascinating building; it was built in 1828 of white Carrara marble, to be the grand entrance to Buckingham Palace.

In the early eighteen-sixties it had to be moved due to road layout. Consisting as it does of three archways, the centre one being the largest and forming part of the Royal Route. Above the arches and in fact the side structures, there are rooms that serve as police rooms for various functions. If you were to stand and face north the support to the left contained a room with a telephone switchboard. This is where the Scottish constables would go to make phone calls home. Further up there was the bathroom and then across the top of the arch a large room that contained odds and ends. Down the other side there was another bathroom and then the superintendents' office which was only ever used for ceremonial occasions. To gain entrance to the interior of the building you used the police key attached to the whistle chain. Now sometimes it was necessary to have privacy especially when you were entertaining someone of the opposite sex. I therefore removed the doorknob and square shaft with it from the entrance door to the senior officers' side of the arch. This I carried about with me and it enabled me to gain access to the superintendents' room without having to go through the ordinary entrance on the other side. I could still use the key for the mortise lock but I had the only means of opening the door. It worked well for some appreciable time.

The main room at the top sounded like an echo chamber and was a very efficient early warning device. I spent many an enjoyable ten minutes or so in that room. I can't remember who I passed the door knob onto but I'm sure they would have put it to good use.

During a riot in 1855 against Lord Grosvenor's Sunday-Trading Bill, a crowd was brought to order by a body of police who emerged from the Arch taking the demonstrators by surprise.

The area in which Marble Arch now stands was known as Tyburn, the site of three-legged gallows, a place of public execution, where crowds gathered to witness the gruesome sight.

One of the things that happened at Marylebone Lane concerned the other relief. A young lady arriving late home from school was admonished by her father who enquired as to her lateness. The young lady said that she had found a ten-shilling note on her way home from school and had handed it to a policeman. The father, being a law-abiding citizen, went to the station to see if it had been handed in. The answer was no, so we now had an allegation of a crime committed by a policeman.

The senior officer in the CID office notified Scotland Yard and a detective chief superintendent was assigned to investigate the matter. The man chosen for this task was the very same man who, a few years before, had investigated corruption between senior police officers, publicans and bookmakers in Brighton, it was Mr Hannam. He duly arrived at Marylebone Lane and interviewed, in turn, all the men that were on duty that day. Such was his aggressive approach to the questioning that he reduced some young policemen to tears. The Police Federation representative was Vic Reece (Shag) who then, as he was quite entitled to do, sat in on the questioning. He was so shocked by Hannam's approach to the whole affair that Vic reported the matter to Superintendent Martin-Smith who, after having words with the officers already questioned, decided that he would look into the matter from another and most important viewpoint: namely, had a crime in fact been committed.

He went to the complainant's address and questioned the girl in the presence of her parents. She admitted that she did not find a ten-shilling note and that she was late home as she had been delayed by meeting her boy-friend. Martin-Smith returned to the station and telephoned the commissioner and explained what had taken place. In consequence Hannam was called to the phone and told, in no uncertain terms, that he was to leave Marylebone at once, which he did. When the two reliefs were together, that is those about to go off duty and those about to start, they apologised for what had taken place and told everyone present that Mr Hannam would never come to the station again.

The basic fault with the investigating officer was that he omitted the cardinal point of an investigation, namely that had a crime in fact been committed. One can imagine what could and most probably would have happened if Martin-Smith had not been such a good policeman: an identification parade and the young lady might possibly have picked anyone out and he would have finished up doing two years in prison.

Hannam's son joined the force and went on to be a very successful and well-liked policeman and climbed the promotional ladder.

Martin-Smith, as chief superintendent, had a very gentlemanly approach to being the governor of the station. If he wanted to see you on a matter in which you could help, he would make a note in the parade book thus: 325 please see the CH. SUP next time parading. If, however, there was trouble looming he would omit the please, and one was then forewarned.

Invariably, in his office you would be offered a glass of sherry and a biscuit. His philosophy was that we as constables were the governors on the streets and we could look to him for support in whatever we did. It was an example of good management and led to a very happy and efficient station.

It was the case that any policeman found committing a crime, however minor, would be charged and if it was a case that the local magistrate could deal with, the guilty policeman would invariably receive a sentence of two years' imprisonment, the maximum that the magistrate could impose. Should the crime be of such a nature that the magistrate could not deliver a suitable sentence then the policeman would be committed to Sessions where a larger sentence could be imposed.

I heard of one policeman at Balham removing a few Green Shield stamps from a stolen car that had been recovered and was in the station yard awaiting collection by its owner. Being caught in the act he was arrested, charged with theft and at the court, sentenced to the almost obligatory two years. The justice in this was that, as policemen, they knew their obligations to society and should be above reproach. One has to remember that, not only do they have the prison sentence to serve, they also, naturally lose their jobs and with it the pension to which they have subscribed, in my day it was six percent of our earnings. There is also the dramatic upheaval they cause to their families. It is quite right that this is the way it worked. Apart from one exception, they were all honest men and took a great pride in being so.

The one exception was a young policeman that was finally transferred to the sticks and then sacked. He had that something about him that made one avoid him like the plague: he had great potential for trouble, a character flaw that became obvious the more one came into contact with him. Finally the job got rid of him.

CORONATION

I was on night duty the night before the Coronation and spent a very enjoyable time with the crowds that began to collect in Oxford Street. There was lots of good natured banter and no incident that warranted any action on my part. Across Oxford Street in a side street close to Bond Street a cafe remained open all night, serving tea and other refreshments to the public. I finished duty at 6 a.m. but went back to join the crowds. Such was the mass of people along this part of the route that when the procession finally appeared I had to stand with a policewoman on the stays of one of the stretchers that was leaning against a wall in order to see the sights. The fact that it began to rain certainly didn't dampen the spirit of the whole day.

The royal revue of police was to take place in Hyde Park and we were sent to Hendon to rehearse for the event. The arrangement was that on the sound of the note 'G' on a bugle we were to come to attention. At Hendon the Marylebone Lane contingent formed up and we were all busy smoking and eating sweets. When we heard this strange noise we all began cheering and making rude noises. After a telling off by the senior officer present, what was finally the note of 'G' was sounded and we came to a sort of attention. We were then marched over the playing field. As we had never heard the note of 'G' before I think we can be forgiven for the cock-up that took place. We recognised the spot where we had moved off from because of the smouldering dog ends and the sweet papers.

Came the big day in Hyde Park and I found myself standing in the second rank next to one of the MacDonalds from Marylebone Lane. As the Queen came by in her Land Rover he took from his pocket a medal case and after opening it pinned on his tunic the DFC. I asked him about this later and he said that as her father had given it to him he only wore it in her company. He had served as a pilot during the war but I never did find out why he was awarded such a medal.

On the parade being finally dismissed I assisted with an elderly constable from one of the constabularies who had collapsed and died from heart failure.

AN EARLY CAR

The Wolseley car normally had an illuminated name badge on the top centre of the radiator grill. With all police cars the bulb had been removed so that we wouldn't give the game away while moving about during the hours of darkness. In those days we didn't need labels on the car to show that it was a police vehicle.

I can remember that the radio log book was being continually filled up with vehicles that had been lost or stolen. What was amazing that one old pre-war policeman had the ability to recall registration numbers of motor vehicles that had been lost or stolen months before and had been recovered and returned to their rightful owners, or not as the case may be. He was instrumental in apprehending many villains in possession of stolen cars.

There were no heaters in these Wolseleys and we were issued with the shorter British warm overcoat which tended, in the close confines of the car, to make you soporific and during slack moments we would often nod off while we were left in the capable hands of the area car driver while he gently cruised over the ground.

Each car had the chrome bell on its front bumper bar and when it was sounded we in the car could hear it but, by their response, the general public were either stone deaf or chose to ignore it.

When I joined Traffic Patrol one of the first cars I was to drive for real, was the Wolseley 6/80 and I found it one of the most pleasant cars to drive.

MY FIRST CORPSE

It was while learning the beats with Bob Gale, a lovely man with great wit, that I saw my first corpse. We were on early turn and at about 9.30 when the female publican at a pub in Bryanston Street called us in as she had realized that her aged mother had died during the night. They had slept together and during the night the daughter had woken up and said, 'Mum, your feet are cold.' Later she woke again and realized that her mother had died. We were shown up to the bedroom where we found the mother half in and half out of the bed. Having sent the daughter out of the room we arranged for her own doctor to be called in to certify her mother's death, and to set about trying to straighten the mother out.

There was no way she could be put into a box in the position she had now set into with her legs spread apart. After about ten minutes we managed to get the old lady into some sort of order, not without a few nervous giggles. We then went downstairs and organized for the Co-op Funeral Service to come and take the lady away, after being examined by the doctor. For our troubles we had a pint of bitter and a packet of fags, before going back to the station to write up our report. I often wondered whether the Co-op Funeral Service gave out dividend stamps and if so, how did one feel when licking them and sticking them in the book?

Bob Gale was an electronic whiz kid, who had made himself a tape recorder before they were available in the shops. We put together one or two comedy sketches with the help of the BBC Sound Effects Department record that might even still be available today. He ended up resigning and went out to New Zealand to join his brother with Macintosh Toffee Company; doing very well for himself, and becoming a manager in the company.

ONE SUNDAY MORNING

I was sent from the station one Sunday morning to a

hotel off Oxford Street where a young lady guest had been found dead in her bath. I was greeted in the foyer by the manager who showed me up to the room but wouldn't go inside as he was too upset by the sight of her. I can well understand why. She was found in the bath, and all that I could see was her long dark hair splayed out on the surface which was covered in vomit. Having put a sheet from the bed on the bedroom floor I lifted her out and laid her on the sheet. I then rang the station to tell them the situation.

The inspector arrived accompanied by the managing director of the hotel who asked the inspector if he'd like a drink. The inspector pointed out that I was the one dealing with the matter and that I should be the one asked that question instead. The hotel manager who had been keeping well to the back was then told to get whatever I wanted. I opted for a brandy and a few moments later he reappeared with a silver tray bearing a small bottle of brandy, a brandy glass and twenty cigarettes.

One of the most important things in dealing with a sudden death is to inform the relatives, but search as we did, we could not find any evidence of her next of kin. We worked out what we thought had happened.

It appeared that she was a Catholic lady of about twenty and from the evidence of an empty gin bottle on the floor we assumed she had indulged herself the night before. We also discovered from her passport that she had returned from Europe the previous day. I assumed that getting up on the Sunday and deciding to attend mass she had climbed into the bath, vomited, choked on it and then slid under the water. This was a very sad incident. I often found that when we had a sudden death, unless the third parties were relatives, the majority of people were quite indifferent to the whole episode and considered it to be a nuisance, which didn't say very much for our so-called caring society.

It was a lovely English summer's day, a Sunday and I'd had a early dinner with my wife at our flat at Formosa Street. I took the underground to Bond Street, walked to the station to find that I was acting sergeant for the late turn. After parading the relief I went up to the front office where the station sergeant introduced me to a member of the Corps of Commissionaires who related that he had a man in his bothy in the foyer of the block of flats who had come along to find his friend who had not come home as he should, and who was employed by tenants as a valet. The man then said that he had gone up to the flat, the tenants being away in the South of France, and had found the valet had hanged himself.

I went with the commissionaire to the block of flats where I had words with the disturbed partner of the valet. His appearance was such that he, bearing mind this was the Fifties, was somewhat bent. I said to him that I gathered his friend was not very well and I would go to him. Leaving the other man in the bothy I went up to the flat where I found a man, the valet, sitting in a chair, between the kitchen and the scullery, with a rope round his neck; this rope had been tied to a vertical exposed pipe over a horizontal pipe and then to the man. What had happened was this: the two men, the one in the bothy and the valet, lived together as homosexuals in Camden Town and had been given notice to quit. The valet had then gone to his employers' flat knowing that they were away and had committed suicide. The nature of his death was confirmed by Francis Camps to me at St Pancras Coroners' Court.

The fact that the corpse had taken on a bit of an odour and that his tongue protruded out of his mouth and was black showed that he had been dead for quite a few hours, in fact about thirty–six. I made my mind up that I would have to reassure the man in the bothy so told him that his friend was very ill and that if he came to Marylebone Police Station in about an hour we would let him know how his friend was. There was a good reason for this: the one thing I didn't want was the living member of the liaison to go out and throw himself under a bus or whatever. Being satisfied he left the bothy and we then set about having the body certified as dead and then having it removed.

I returned to the station and told the sergeant what had transpired and told him that he would be having a queer come to the station and he had to inform him that his partner was dead. There were facilities there for comforting him, for example a quiet chat and a cup of tea. None of these were available at the block of flats. At the inquest at St Pancras Coroners' Court I apologised for the lie I had told him. He accepted it in good grace and stated that he would have done the same thing if he had been in my position.

Francis Camps said to me that as the man stepped off the chair and the ligature round his neck had tightened he became a dead lump and sank into the chair as his weight caused the rope round the vertical pipe to slide up.

MAGISTRATES

There were two magistrates that come readily to mind when I remember my days at Marylebone Lane. There was Paul Bennett VC: white haired with a ruddy complexion. He never stood any nonsense in his court at Marlborough Street and was a kind and understanding man. He defended 'his policemen' from unfair cross-examination.

Rowland Thomas also sat at the same court. He was a short, round man who loved his cricket, so much so that when there was a test match on at Lords he would have the local area car at the back of the court building waiting to whisk him up there at the completion of the morning's business.

The business consisted of prostitutes and drunks alternately. They would enter the court in turn, with the arresting officer and the clerk of the court would take the pleas. If it was a guilty plea the officer gave his evidence and the magistrate would impose a fine. In the case of drunks this normally took the form of all the loose change he had in his pocket and if he was completely broke he spent one day in custody as a penalty, which meant that at about twelve noon and a meal he would be let out. The prostitutes were invariably fined forty shillings for soliciting and back they went to work!

The Australians were at Lords when Roland Thomas, on seeing a new defendant in the dock said, 'Fined forty shillings'. The clerk had to point out to him that a plea hadn't been taken. Such was his need to get to Lords.

He was so short that his feet didn't touch the floor when he sat in the magistrates chair and he covered his legs with a police blanket. These blankets were blue and maroon striped things and invariably covered the back seats of senior officers' cars.

FLAT FIRE

One night I was walking along Paddington Street with Johnny Swallow. Johnny always wore his macintosh open with one hand in his pocket and his helmet slightly tilted to one side with his chin strap tucked underneath, and never without a cigarette in his mouth. This attire would be worn on night duty of course. During the daylight hours he was slightly more respectable. We heard the sound of a fire engine coming up Marylebone High Street, so I quickened my pace, but Johnny Swallow said, 'Slow down, it will still be burning when you get there.'

We found that a fire in a flat on Devonshire Street had been so intense that the plaster on the walls had disappeared, as had the glass from the metal window frames. The fire had happened in the bedroom and had blistered the paint on the flat hallway and the wall of the communal corridor. The only objects left in the bedroom were the metal remains of the bed and the burnt body of an eight month pregnant woman. She was so burned that it had consumed her hands and feet and the features on her face had gone.

The ambulance crew that attended refused to take her to University College Hospital. I pointed out that neither they nor I were qualified to certify her dead. They took her in the end after we lifted her onto a rubber sheet with shovels. Her estranged husband came up from, I think, Chislehurst and insisted, against my advice, on looking at the burnt out room. He left the flat in tears and drove off at a fast speed.

I discovered that Johnny Swallow and the Inspector Reg Court, a small gentle gentleman of the caring sort, were up on the flat roof of the block having a glass of scotch with one of the residents. Reg Court complimented me on the way I had dealt with the matter and insisted that I joined him for a scotch. He also said that I had been such a good boy that I could enter my report up in the occurrence book at the station. Normally the sergeant at the station did this so I suppose he thought it would be a little treat for me.

It was the following day that a report of the fire was in the London evening papers. I don't know which one it was, either the Standard or the Evening News, stated that she had been rushed to hospital in an effort to save her unborn child. Such is the freedom of the press, the other paper was more factual and didn't attempt to sensationalize. I often wonder what the poor husband must have felt on reading such utter nonsense.

I made a mistake when I went to the section house for a meal that night. I had a pork brawn salad, and the sight of it brought back such memories that I couldn't eat it. The fact that the smell remained on my uniform for days wasn't a great help either.

I developed a feel for the sadness of others, when they had suffered bereavement in the family, which stayed with me throughout my career. More especially the sudden accidental death of a child was always an emotional problem for the policemen or women who had to deal with the matter.

NOT THE ORIENTAL CARPET!

One of the most popular crimes committed against stores in Oxford Street was to hide in the building near closing time and then during the night have a complete change of clothes and when the store opened up in the morning the villain of the piece would walk out. That was the idea, and a very poor one it was too. We would often get the call that there were suspects on the premises. This happened at Selfridges one night. We all went round to the rear of the building in the mews where the food hall now stands and waited for the dog handler with his dog to arrive from Hyde Park. As soon as he arrived we were let in to search the building. The first thing the dog did on arriving at the Oriental Carpet Department was to cock his leg up on one of the more expensive items of merchandise to relieve himself.

No suspect was found that night, but we had a most enjoyable hour in the warm, sitting in the ladies' hairdressing department. Such incidents added to the boring passing of time during the hours of darkness.

THE FRENCH WAY

Night duty on the beat in Oxford Street was very different in the Fifties than I gather it would be today. There were very few people about and invariably most were caterers, bakers and waiters on their way home. It was said that the only people about in the real early hours of the morning were poofs, ponces, prostitutes and policemen.

A very well dressed lady was walking along the north side of the road going towards Marble Arch. Now it was always my view that I should make myself aware of those people passing through my beat at such a time, so I decided to pass the time of day with her and she said in a glorious French accent that she was a business girl and did it 'the French Way.' I pleaded ignorant so she told me what this was and invited me to partake. We finished up in the mews behind Selfridges where there were cast iron stairs leading to a flat. Half way up the stairs was a landing where we stood, or rather where I stood and was shown how the French really like to have their way. During the following weeks this took place at irregular intervals. It was during one of these treats in the side doorway of DH Evans on Henrietta place, which was not named after me I don't believe, that the night watchman from that store walked past and said, 'Good night, officer.'

Vic Reece, otherwise known as Shag Reece, who had received his name for the normal biological function of the procreation of species, and getting his end away on many occasion with many a fine girl, came in and said, 'You dirty lucky ucker.' Shag Reece was the van driver on my relief and he was always looking for the funny side of things.

Superintendent Martin-Smith was a very good governor, he used to say to everybody, 'You're the governor on the streets and I'm the governor in the station. Whatever you do in the street I'll back you up.'

He would always inform us if we were going to get a bollocking, ahead of time.

Supt Martin-Smith approached me in the foyer of the station and asked me if there were any prostitutes on the ground because one hadn't been arrested for quite some time and the book for recording such events looked a little bare. I said that I hadn't seen one for some time, so he told me to get the van driver and go out and get us one. We drove down Oxford Street: not a sign of one So off our ground and onto Paddington, down Bayswater Road which was usually a good spot for them, but again no luck. We finished up at Notting Hill Gate where we finally caught up with one, standing on the street corner, wearing Grecian sandals and swinging her handbag. Shag stopped the van and told her she was nicked. She replied, 'I was nicked the other night.' Shag said, 'Well you're nicked again.'

She climbed into the back of the van. She said that she hadn't seen us about before, and we explained that we were from a very nice police station, Marylebone Lane. Shag explained to her that she would be charged, bailed and we would run her back to Notting Hill Gate. She was a big busted girl and it was explained to her by Shag that when she entered the charge room she should give a quick flash to the sergeant and then she would be on her way back to her place of work in no time at all. What Shag didn't mention was that the sergeant who would be charging her was a bit of a tit himself. When we arrived at the station, Shag took the young lady through to the charge room. I went into the front office to explain to the sergeant that we had arrested a prostitute. He picked up the charge book sheet, a pen and ink, and walked through to the charge room. As soon as he entered she did indeed give him a nice flash of her beautiful firm breasts to which he then screamed, 'Put her in the cell, I'll no' deal with her tonight.' Shag also failed to mention that Sergeant Catto, a Scot, was a member of the Plymouth Brethren and had no tolerance for such behaviour. 'You bastards,' she screamed, and we put her in the cell for the night to be dealt with the next day.

Night duty during the Fifties at Marylebone Lane was not a tedious task. Having ambled round your beat or beats you checked that everything was in order. When you first went on duty at ten o'clock there were still people out and about and as the night wore on they would gradually thin out until in the early hours you might not find anyone about.

The forty-five minute meal break was taken at either the station or at the section house that had a night shift of catering staff, possibly just one lady who would serve you and prepare the meal. Some nights at the station Reg Brind would take any stray dog for a walk up Wigmore Street to Portman Square as he had a key to the private gardens there. He would let the dog have a good run round while he sat in the summer house relaxing and enjoying a cigarette. Then back to the station with the dog which in the morning would be taken to Battersea Dogs home to await an uncertain fate.

At four in the morning there would be many policemen making their way to the station for an unofficial tea break where everybody could be accounted for. After that once more round your entire beat or beats and then at about a quarter to six make your way again to the station to book off duty.

Before making your way to the station for the cup of tea you might, especially at the top end of the ground, meet up with a colleague and walk to the station together. At Marylebone Circus at the top end of Baker Street we often met up with a young lady of the night making her way home. She would have the day's daily papers with her and would share them out. We would often have a friendly chat with her before we made our way to the station.

During your patrol round the various streets you would find a place, say for example a deep doorway where you could shelter from the elements and have a quiet smoke and at the same time watch for any movement going on. This was more essential when winter set in. If there was a frost on the ground and perhaps even snow, it was nice to know that you could find your way to your hidey-hole and get some protection from the elements. Then again if I saw a woman walking alone during the middle of the night I would always say hello and walk with her until she was off my beat, so that she knew that help was there in the form of the policeman patrolling his ground. In this way the nights passed on but there was the rare time when I thought what the bloody hell am I doing walking about in the dark, wet through, when everybody else was warm in bed and fast asleep? It quickly passed, this moment of doubt, and at the end of the shift, back at the section house I would have a good wash, clean my teeth and then to bed.

THE TARDIS

Commonly referred to now by avid fans and non-fans of the hit science-fiction BBC TV show Dr Who, 'The Tardis' is also known as a police box, which was first introduced to Britain in 1888, originating from the United States.

The first Tardis-like box materialized in Newcastle in the north-east of England in 1929 and by 1937 there was an extensive network of boxes all over England. Police boxes were large blue kiosks topped by an electric flashing light which was there to indicate to patrolling officers that they were required to make contact with the station.

Each box contained a stool, a table, some brushes and dusters, a fire extinguisher and sometimes a very inadequate electric fire. The telephones were linked directly to the local sub- divisional police station, so officers on their beat could check in and wouldn't have to make carefully timed meetings with their sergeants, and of course to report any incidents. All the boxes were locked and we had the key to the boxes on our whistle chain.

One night, Shag Reece met up with a woman of the night and had been seen by Reg Court and Sergeant Pennington being given 'one off the wrist' whilst lurking in a doorway. They were such gentleman that they would never have disturbed his pleasures but the following night he found himself reposted to thirteen and a half, [??040] eleven beat, which was right up the top of the grounds close to Marylebone Station. Later that night it must have dawned on him that this was the reason for this repost. That night he again ended up with some young lady and took her back in the police box. He called the station at the time when we were all on our refreshment break playing cards. He put the girl on the phone and had her describe everything he was doing to her. We were all huddled together listening in on the dirty old boy. Shag had taken total advantage of the bad post he had been given, from being a naughty boy the night before, and was truly living up to his name.

The police box was used for many different things as well as the above mentioned, if it wasn't just for a quick smoke to get away from it all, it would also double up as a holding cell for a prisoner till the van came around to pick him, or quite possibly her, up. The police boxes were later ditched in favour of walkie-talkies in 1969. I'm sure there are a few boxes scattered about today, if not in working order I'm sure made into art and displayed in museums or on old reruns of Dr Who.

THE DRUNKEN SCOTSMAN

I was on duty at Marble Arch doing the 10 a.m.–6 p.m. shift, when a drunken Scotsman came to my notice. He was threatening everyone within earshot so I arrested him and walked him down Oxford Street toward the station; I think it was about midday. In Wigmore Street he continued threatening to give me a bunch of fives and I kept telling him he was welcome to try. I should have called for the van to take him to the station, but there was no way I could have held him and used the police post at Marble Arch. Anyway, just before we got to Duke Street he swung at me, I swung at him and we landed on the path with my helmet in the road. As I stuck my knee in his groin, a bus driver jumped out of his bus and asked if I needed any help, which was very nice of him, but I told him that I was OK. I reprimanded the Scotsman and pointed out the error of his ways. At the station he was charged with being drunk and disorderedly and was taken to Marylebone Street Magistrates' Court where he was disposed of. All the cash he had on him was about four shillings, which would only be about 25p in today's money. This was kept as a fine, and he was held in the cell until he sobered up.

It was always reassuring that help would be forthcoming from the general public, although there were always those who would stand by and do nothing. Prostitutes were the greatest of support in a brawl and would wade in on behalf of the constable and always gave a very good account of themselves. Handbag swinging, obscenities being shouted, they were great allies to have in a time of need.

TO THINK THIS COULD HAPPEN IN LONDON

Jock Begg, a Scottish fellow constable and I, had gone down to Victoria for a drink one evening. I think we ended up at The Volunteer, close to Victoria Place. We were invited, or we invited ourselves, to sit with these two young ladies who were already quite merry from drink. The one with spots and glasses Jock finished up with, while I opted for the more attractive and clear complexioned one. Their conversation was a little disjointed, but the gist of it was that the attractive one was at last a free woman in the world again. Apparently her divorce had been granted and they were out celebrating. At the end of the evening I took my young lady home to Streatham, where she lived in a very nice flat in the High Road. We had coffee and she chatted away for some appreciable time about her ex-husband who was apparently a film producer. She was working at the Times Bookshop on Wigmore Street which was about a hundred yards from Marylebone Lane. As I was late turn the following day I arranged to meet her outside the bookshop, and spend the rest of the evening with her. On the coffee table was a photograph of her daughter, who was spending a few days with her grandmother. As the time was now quite late and public transport non-existent she suggested that I stayed and slept on the sofa. She went off to bed, moving a small table out of the way so that I wouldn't fall over it. After a short while I ended up joining her in her bed and slept deeply for the rest of the night. In the morning she suggested that I could stay in bed while she went to work. I was to help myself to breakfast and let myself out, which I did. I left the flat around 8.30 a.m. and was greeted by the cleaning lady in the hallway who wished me a good morning.

That afternoon when I went on duty, I asked for four hours off but we were already short manned and so I was refused. Sadly the date with the young lady had to be cancelled and she passed out of my life.

Three weeks later the headlines of the Daily Mirror read, 'To Think This Could Happen in London.' With a front page spread showing the front of the block of flats in Streatham, and the photograph of the young lady with her daughter, the same as I had seen in the flat. She had been found dead. After the paper and milk had accumulated outside her flat for about a fortnight, someone had gone in to investigate, finding her lying on the bed in her underclothes. Assessing the situation I felt it best to keep quiet about my spending the night in her flat weeks earlier. Some days later it was reported that she had died from an overdose and was suffering from TB.

To this day I regret that I didn't pursue her or call on her at her place of work to maintain our young but possibly blooming relationship. It could have only been the traumatic divorce and the illness that had driven her to take her own life, and the absence of a good friend to turn to I'm sure had not helped either.

I spoke of this with Jock Begg and was very saddened by the whole occurrence.

THE GOLDEN RULE

On night duty one had to check every door on the beat, both on going on duty and before the completion of the shift. I once worked out from an ordinance survey map that I had walked about sixteen miles during each night on one particular beat. Sometimes you would find a door open and if it was business premises, the station was informed, and the key holder asked to attend to make the premises secure. We would often have to search the place with the key holder to ensure that everything was in order.

Private dwellings were another matter. I found a door open in Chiltern Street and so searched the place and found this couple in bed. I didn't disturb them but swiftly and quietly left, closing the door behind me.

On another occasion I discovered an au-pair awake sitting up in bed, topless, with a look of amazement that a policeman had walked into her room. I explained that the flat door was open and again left quietly.

In the old days you had to mark the premises with various means to ensure that the place hadn't been broken into during the night. Through these duties you got to know the ground very well indeed; the fact that you had to look after at least one beat, possibly as many two during the night, improved your local knowledge and made for a better policeman.

EMBASSY ANTICS

During the 1950s the problem with Cyprus blew up, embarking on the struggle for independence. Various threats were made between the Greeks, Turks and the British. As we had the Turkish Embassy on our ground we were involved in its protection. In fact we had a permanent posting outside the building situated on Devonshire Street at the corner of Great Portland Place. Not only did we have to stand outside the place for eight hours, we were also armed and carried a Webley 38 revolver, with a loaded cylinder and six spare rounds in a buff envelope. The fact that the rounds were covered in verdigris, and that we had had no instruction on the use of the weapon, and more importantly when to use it, meant the whole episode was fraught with potential danger.

We had the use of a toilet in the area of the Embassy just under the pavement, and I would sit on the throne with my trousers down examining this tool of destruction.

We developed a pattern of walking up and down becoming thoroughly bored. One or two of the lads developed an affinity for the young female residents of the neighbourhood and one was in fact literally caught with his trousers down by the grandmother of the young lady in question. On trying to pull them up, the truncheon pocket complete with truncheon went across the crutch making it impossible to do so. The young lady was told by her grandmother to have nothing more to do with the naughty policeman, but of course she did.

I was on night duty there during a snowstorm and had myself the task of putting up the Union Jack in the snow, which was six inches deep.

A little later on I was hit in the head by a snowball and couldn't see where it had come from. I was then hit by another one and discovered Shag Reece had climbed on to a statue in Great Portland Place and was busy manufacturing further snow balls to throw at me. How he managed to climb up there I'll never know; even to this day when I'm passing by the statue I still can't work out how he managed it.

One of the essential things to do was to see that people didn't loiter outside the Embassy building. I know on one occasion there was a lady hanging outside the Embassy and I politely asked her to move on, which was what I was there for. She became most indignant and had assumed that I thought she was a lady of the street. She was in fact the secretary to Simpson, the Home Office Pathologist who arrived after a few minutes and walked her on her way. He did have a few words with me to explain that she was going through that funny time of the month. I recorded the incident in my pocketbook and mentioned it to Martin-Smith when I was next in the station, who also commented on the nature of the irrationality of women.

The Ambassador had a new American car delivered which was kept in the garage. It was an automatic, and the son of the Ambassador, a lad about twelve years old got into the sparkling new car, started up the engine and shot it straight into the garage wall causing a fair bobs' worth of damage. The chauffeur wasn't too pleased either, as you could well imagine, and the young lad kept himself to himself for the rest of his time there.

OOPS!

We had a cricket team at Marylebone Lane named the Marylebone Lane Ramblers, and once a year we would play the ground staff at Lords on the nursery ground there. The previous years they had played on the main cricket square but the members had suggested that our cricket attire was not one hundred percent and we should be relegated to the other place.

Stan Bassham, a pre-war copper and an idle bugger, was a great cricketer and during the cold, wet, wintry months would be found secretly in a small room next to the plan drawer's room in the top of the building oiling the bats. Well that's what he said he was doing if he was ever found by the sergeant or inspector. In fact Stan would freely admit to being idle. In all his years on the service he had only ever arrested one man and only because it was forced on him in the following manner.

He was on night duty sitting on a dustbin in a mews having a smoke, when a bag whistled past his ear. He said he wouldn't have minded but the burglar coming over the wall then put his foot on Stan's shoulder while searching for the step down via the dustbin. Stan had no other choice than to arrest him. His writing was shocking. It was as if a spider had fallen into a bottle of ink and had then walked over a piece of paper. He used to say that if he never put pen to paper then he would never get in trouble. That is the way Stan chose to live his life.

WASN'T ME, DIDN'T DO IT!

One night I was walking a young lady home through my beat when we decided to look for somewhere to have a smoke. I suggested that we just climb into the back of this van that was parked there. I helped her up first then climbed up myself, had one last look around to see if the coast was clear and when I turned back to her she was completely undressed and laying on her back right on the dust sheets. Well in these circumstances I only had to take my helmet off and go along for the ride.

Night duty was not always full of such sexual adventures although if you missed a couple of nights without some invitation you felt hard done by and wondered who you should complain to. I suppose the fact that one was young and wearing the uniform of a constable had a certain attractiveness for the more amorous females on Marylebone Lane's ground and we were not a potential threat to them.

A young lady came into the station one day to tell the sergeant that one of the policemen had made her pregnant. When asked to describe him she couldn't remember his number but just that he'd had a moustache. Well the following day there wasn't a moustache to be seen in the station, except for the old pre-war coppers who were definitely not at risk.

DIRTY BUGGERS BRIGADE

One of the problems that we had to deal with during the normal shopping hours was that of street traders. Most of them operated from a suitcase on the pavement outside Selfridges and sold jewellery, scarves, and other small, high priced, quick return items. They would have a crowd gathered round and it was this that constituted the offence of obstructing the pavement.

You had to move quick to catch them, for once they saw a police helmet approaching, their suitcases were shut and they disappeared into the crowd.

One such was Bernard Kirby, who, whenever he was caught would show you the mass of summonses he had accumulated since his last appearance at court. They paid their fines and resumed trading, putting the fines down as a necessary business expense. We seldom had complaints from the general public about the items they had purchased; they paid their money and took their chances.

In the big stores when I was patrolling with a colleague in plain clothes, we would often discover the 'Bustle Puncher' at work. He would come up behind a crowd of woman at a demonstration and finding what appeared to be a likely source of delight, would, through the pocket of his raglan type raincoat, push his hand against the bottom of his target and move it about. Most women would turn on him and move away but I can remember one young female standing and obviously enjoying it. It was his lucky day until I tapped him on the shoulder and marched him out of the store.

It was the same type of raincoat that served the pickpockets as a tool of their trade; their hand would remove the purse from the top of the shopping bag and then secretly put it in their jacket pocket under the mac. This was also the same mackintosh that the Dirty Buggers Brigade wore, and was conveniently designed for flashing.

One gentleman I watched in Selfridges appeared to be looking at the ground but was in fact looking up ladies' skirts using a small mirror which was fixed to the end of a telescopic car aerial. What delight he found in doing this and the fact that when I arrested him I discovered that he was an airline pilot for BOAC, at the time made me suspicious of the moral standards of such people that still remains with me to this day.

The stock answer given by all perverts that I had dealings with was that they were having treatment. What this consisted of I do not know because most appeared to have gone into relapse.

It takes all sorts, and without such deviants and with everybody law abiding, life for a young policeman in the West End in the early Fifties would have been quite boring.

TOM, DICK AND HARRY

During the evening and early part of the night, the prostitutes were busy in Hyde Park and the top end of Park Lane. Most of the nitty-gritty of the sexual intercourse took place against the trees, mostly London Plane, in the park, with the hangers-on, slipping through the park ever watchful and the peeping toms keeping themselves busy too.

Many young Irishmen acted as minders for the toms and would be rewarded by the occasional half-a-crown. Most of their day was spent sleeping on the grass. For meals and other light refreshments they would go to Bickards Café just at the bottom of Edgware Road and would then congregate outside the café.

It was while learning beats that we came upon such a group, spread across the pavement and causing a bit of a nuisance. The pre-war constable I was with asked the group who had been there the longest. Paddy steps forward and says, 'Me, sir.' We then accompanied him to the rear end of the old Odeon where he was given a firm clout around the ear and told to fuck off and take his mates with him. We then slowly walked round the block and when we came back, the pavement outside Bickards would of course be clear. I was assured that this was the only way to deal with the problem and had we chosen to ask them jointly to move on the least we could have expected was abuse and possibly a punch up. The approach used had certainly done its job and on future evenings the group only had to see a policeman coming towards them to disperse.

NODDY

One young man joined Marylebone Lane about three years after me. His name was Jones and for the following reason was given the nickname Noddy. He had a nervous habit of always nodding his head, so much so that the members of the public would often call the station to say that there was a policeman having a fit. Not to mention he was a complete and utter prat. We all tried to avoid him because he was a continual source of embarrassment. I heard him shout obscenities across Baker Street in broad daylight with everyone milling about; to say that a few eyebrows were raised would be putting it mildly. We all reasoned that as he was Welsh and as the Home Secretary was Bevin, he must have pulled a few strings to get him the job or to put it another way they got the wrong Jones.

He was eventually transferred out of the West End to the sticks down Surbiton way. Once established there, he found his way into the local youth club and wanted to demonstrate self-defence; a subject he new absolutely nothing about. He handed his truncheon to some young lad and invited him to attack him. The young lad did, and with great success as one blow to the head laid Noddy out. Thus what a prat.

SNOOKER

While I was aid to CID, during the lunch hour we would play snooker in the basement of the station. One day three of us were waiting for a fourth player to appear so that we could have a game of doubles when this new lad came into the snooker room. We invited him to make up our foursome and play a game for a shilling a corner. He told us that he would love to play but wouldn't play for money. Now as half the fun was the chance of taking a shilling off your mate by your superior snooker playing, we assumed he must be religious or something. Anyway the game got going after we talked him into having a wager. The three of us played our shots and the newcomer came to the table and cleared the lot. It turned out it he was Graham Miles who went on to be the UK Police Champion and became a professional with great success. As we spent so much time at the section house we would often practise together and it was because of him that my snooker improved.

'PARK PLAZA 605'

They were shooting a film called 'Park Plaza 605' in Cavendish Square with Tom Conway, the moustached brother of George Sanders, playing the lead. Tom Conway's action was to drive a Sunbeam Alpine Coupe round the corner and stop outside a derelict house. The house had its windows cleaned and a brass name plate fixed to the wall by the front door. The fact that the house hadn't been used since the middle of the war was not apparent after they dressed it up. The producer's caravan was parked by the centre of the square opposite the rear of John Lewis. I was asked to hold up traffic when a signal was given.

Tom Conway was wearing the obligatory trench coat, with all the straps tied up and not through the buckles provided, which was the norm in the Fifties as films of that period show. He drove the car around the corner, stopping outside the building. The first take he forgot to switch off the engine and so when he got out it rolled forward about three feet. The next take he stopped the car got out and forgot to close the door. This kept up until he finally got it right. After all that palaver they all buggered off to their next location.

I can now understand the cost of filming when it takes the star all day to stop a car and walk away from it. Now on screen, even though I never did see the film, I'm sure they made it look like he never did anything wrong and him look most competent.

We had several stars of screen, stage and radio living on our ground and I found them all to be the most pleasant of people to talk to. Most admitted that that they did it for the money, but the occupation carried a certain style with it. The thought of becoming an actor had run through my mind once or twice, but the kind of work I was involved in did allow me, from time to time, to do a certain amount of acting, which came with the job.

FOG

Fog was a big problem in the Fifties. It would come down and reduce visibility to zero. I could be walking on my beat without knowing where I was at any particular time. You would have to take a guess at it and were never quite certain. The only way to find out would be by identifying a shop front or individual window display.

Traffic came to a standstill, although buses still tried to run and so we helped them the best we could by guiding them around Marble Arch to either Bayswater Road or Edgware Road but even then some of them finished up in Hyde Park.

On one occasion the LTE supplied wax flares to help guide them, which we had to hold in our hands and with hot wax dripping all over our greatcoats or macs. I spent days trying to pick the wax off before taking it into the dry cleaners.

At Marble Arch I had a photographer, from the now defunct Daily Sketch, ask if he might take my picture, which I agreed to and it appeared in the following day's paper; not a very good likeness due to all that fog, but at least I knew it was me.

Shop breaking was quite popular at this time too. You could hear the windows breaking but you didn't know what had been broken into, and had to proceed slowly towards the origin of the sound. Opportunists were out getting a head start.

At the old people's home off Paddington Street the ambulance was there daily, together with the local undertaker's van, due to the elderly having succumbed to the effect of the fog. I was coughing up what could only be described as black treacle, it tasted of smoke and was most unpleasant.

The fog permeated everywhere, into the station and section house, you just couldn't get away from it. The lines on your face were grimed with soot and your nostrils needed reaming out to get rid of the muck. We would have a few days of this and then the wind would blow it away and things would return to normal.

PILCHARDS FOR BREAKFAST

One crime that was quite common in the Fifties and perhaps is still today is that known as the 'Short Firm' business. A villain sets himself up as a business and orders goods from a supplier. In the case that I shall now relate the gentleman in question ordered a lorry load of pilchards, in tins of course. He purchased them from somewhere in the west where pilchards come from. Once they were delivered, they were moved onto other premises and the invoice and the other on-going demands for payment ignored and in fact were never received because the villain had already done a runner. He then set about selling his recently acquired stock.

Anyway he was arrested by the CID and the remaining stock of pilchards were recovered and placed in the cell at Marylebone Lane which was used as a secure property place for CID.

At the completion of the case a chap came up from the original suppliers to collect his property. We all helped load the cases of pilchards onto the lorry and there were about a dozen left when we were told that the rest were for us as a reward for doing a good job, which was a very nice gesture. We all ended up going home that night and for many nights to follow with pilchards stuffed in our pockets. We were all stock piled with the buggers and in the end they were reluctantly consumed. Tell you the truth we were fed up with the sight of them. The taste and smell still brings back memories of that and those days after.

'NICE SUIT!' 'THANKS, YOU TOO'

We often had a visit from the Flying Squad, who to my young eyes had a magical quality about them. They came in their smart suits, always going after the big boys in the criminal world. I know that on one occasion they were dealing with the theft of a quantity of cloth from a warehouse, and about a fortnight later they came back to the station all wearing the same suits. Oh well, it must have just been a coincidence.

IT'S A FAIR COP

The Fifties were the days of the Murder Squad, when a detective inspector and sergeant would leave Scotland Yard with their murder bag to assist in the investigation of murders in the counties. There was still capital punishment in those days and murders were crimes that aroused the public and were front page news for many days.

We had a sad murder when the caretaker of a new block of flats drowned his fifteen year old daughter in the bath on the break-up of his marriage and then walked into Marylebone Lane to report it himself. The only light-hearted thing about this episode was that the sergeant who was first approached by the man had no idea what form he should fill in.

BONFIRE NIGHT

On Bonfire Night some of us had to perform duty in Trafalgar Square, mainly to keep order. One student was arrested for being in possession of an RAF flare, about three feet long. If we hadn't caught this person and he had managed to ignite it, there could have been many people seriously injured or even possibly killed. Another idiot was arrested for throwing fireworks into passing cars and onto buses.

Quite a few policemen were set upon, so when trying to help your mates you kept your truncheon out and used it in a stabbing way to keep the aggressive bastards back.

One group of policemen were surrounded and being attacked by a rowdy group who were trying to throw them into the fountains. Three of us fought our way through to them to relieve some of the pressure and force the crowd back. It was in these circumstances where we were closely confined that people did hit out at you.

Now another golden rule is that if anyone strikes Jim, he hits them back, but harder. This I did on about four times that night and they all backed away when they saw that I was not having any nonsense. Happy Bonfire Night indeed.

I was asleep at Elliott House one night when I was awoken by the most horrible and piercing of screams. It sounded as if someone had fallen into a boiling vat of oil. It sounded very close by so I went out in the corridor and found other chaps out there who had heard it too. We searched everywhere but found nothing. If it had been a scream of delight I would have understood but it clearly wasn't.

A guest at the Cumberland Hotel at the corner of Cumberland Place had reported hearing a scream on another night, so looked everywhere. Even the night porter couldn't find anything. However the following day the maintenance men at the hotel discovered a body in one of the air shafts. The roof of the hotel was flat and the air shaft went down through it with no protective barriers round it. To the rear of the hotel just across the road was the female staff quarters and what had happened was that a peeping tom was on the roof moving about to see what he could see and had stepped into one of the air shafts and fell to his death. So I've always said, 'Crumpet will always get you into trouble.'

THE TOP HAT

Marylebone Lane has seen some changes over the years. If you were to walk down Marylebone High Street you would enter Thayer Street at its southern end. You would then come to Wigmore Street which travels from east to west, and crossing over you would come to Marylebone Lane. Almost immediately on your left was the police station. If you were to carry on walking you would see that Marylebone Lane splits into two: the east one runs down to Oxford Street on the west side off Henrietta Place, while the other continues directly to Oxford Street. In the good old days way before London sprawled all over the place there used to be a toll gate, in what is now Oxford Street. The law-abiding people went through the toll gate and paid their dues, which would have been so much per sheep or something like that. Now if people were on their own and a bit scandalous they would duck through the hedges behind the toll gate to save their pennies, hence the two Marylebone Lanes.

Red Brind was a tall well-built man and had been at Marylebone Lane for over twenty years. We were close to the station in Marylebone Lane one evening on our beat, and while we were out Reg found a collapsible top hat. As we stood in a doorway a young couple came walking towards us on their way home. As they passed by Reg took off his helmet and put on the top hat just as the young lady looked round. She then tugged on her boyfriend's arm for him to see this rare sight. He looked round in which time Reg had his helmet back on and the top hat off. It sounded like the chap said, 'Silly bugger,' to the girl. When she looked round for the second time Reg had the top hat back on.

WHIPS AND CHAINS

Often one would be posted to the area car, a Wolseley 6/80 and then would be operating on both Marylebone Lane and Paddington Green's ground.

It was early turn and coming up to midday when we were called to a sudden death in Cambridge Court, a block of flats at the corner of Edgware Road and Sussex Gardens. When we arrived there we found a Hungarian maid who could hardly speak English and her employer who was well into her eighties and dead, on the floor, in the bedroom. We arranged for the local coroner's officer to attend. Then we set about finding who the old lady was and who her relatives were so that we could inform them. We searched the flat and discovered that years previously the old lady had been a prostitute of a very high order and had at one time been a European countess. Under her bed we found a large parcel wrapped in brown paper, which on opening it we discovered contained beautiful leather-bound books of the obscene type. All the gentlemen portrayed in the photographs had moustaches while their partners wore white stockings rolled down below the knee.

All the time we were there the maid was buzzing about more interested in her own future than the death of her employer. I suppose in the circumstances it was only natural as she was an illegal immigrant and her future didn't look too bright.

We also found paraphernalia that went with her previous occupation; whips, handcuffs and all the other things that would now fall under the name of bondage.

We didn't however find out the details of any relatives or indeed anyone we could inform about her demise. After the coroner's officer had come and made his arrangements to have the body removed I volunteered to hang on until this had been done as we did not wish to leave the maid alone with the corpse. It was now nearly two o'clock in the afternoon and we should have been off duty at that time. I stayed anyway and shared some roast duck, green peas and new potatoes with the maid. It transpired that the old lady had committed suicide and that nobody was found that would be in the slightest bit interested in her death.

QUITE THE ARTIST

At the top of Marylebone Lane was the Plan Drawer's Office occupied by the plan drawer Vic Thorpe, a slightly built man and a master of his craft.

I became his assistant, having a slight artistic way about me, and would prepare plans for the various cases, mainly motoring, that would come before the courts. All the lettering had to be done by hand with a mapping pen. We didn't even have Letraset in those days, let alone computers. The overall impression was that they were works of art in their own right and drawn with a degree of accuracy that would and could be tested in the highest courts in the land. I had to certify at the bottom that, I, James Goodwin, a Constable of The Metropolitan Police, had drawn this plan and that it had been accurately drawn to such and such a scale, and then sign it.

I would often be called out to accompany a raid on the premises where the officer in charge would need a plan made up and measurements taken at the time of the raid and not when someone had had time to move things about. I would receive a phone call to tell me to be at a certain police station with my tape and note pad.

I had the job of drawing the plan of a room on Paddington grounds where a prostitute had been murdered with an axe. I had to draw all the various marks, blood splashes and things like that to show their exact sizes. Although a man was arrested for the crime, I wasn't required to attend the Old Bailey as the plans I had prepared were accepted by the defence.

I did one or two bits of private work for senior officers too. I had to draw a plan for the garden of the Chief Inspector's house at Muswell Hill, which earned me some tobacco; a two ounce tin of St. Bruno Flake. He and his wife were so impressed by it they had it framed and hung it in their lounge.

On another occasion I was asked to visit a pub near Westbourne Drive were the publican friend of another senior officer, both Freemasons, had a man fall down the cellar steps mistaking the doorway for the entrance of the gents. A civil action was in the offering but it must have been settled amicably because I heard no more about it.

When the plan drawer at St John's Wood took his annual leave I was attached there for the fortnight. He had been up to date with all his work and I found that most of my time was spent walking about in Regents Park. To cover myself I would leave a pencilled note on the drawing board saying, 'Out to measure up.'

It was pleasant at the time to explore parts of the metropolis.

One of the jobs I had to do as plan drawer was to prepare a scale plan of the whole of Harley Street in order to study the feasibility of the parked vehicles being in echelon formation and not toe to tail along the kerb. This was a direct result of a suggestion made by a member of the public and although a very good idea, when drawn the plan showed that due to the varying lengths of the types of car parking in that salubrious neck of the woods the idea was not a practical one and was rejected. I spent one morning in the street measuring the length of the vehicles there. There were minis to Rolls Royces and the occasional battleship sized American car. I don't know what the public thought to see me doing that; I certainly got some queer looks.

I also had to prepare a plan at the rear of John Lewis's to show the available parking while there was substantial building work going on there. Plans when prepared were drawn on a first class cartridge paper with all the lettering done in fine style. This was then sent off to the photographic section at Scotland Yard to be copied, for some trials as many as a dozen would be requested. At the court, be it coroners', magistrates' or Assize, after taking the oath and swearing that I had prepared the plan I would hand the original plan on the cartridge paper to be handed to the judge or coroner while the photocopies were handed to the counsel and to the jury. I would then have to give my evidence as plan drawer and be subject to cross examination. This was seldom of an unpleasant nature and often meant only clarifying some point or other.

At one coroners' court I would go into the coroner's room before the inquest to go over the plan with him so that he was clear in his mind when it came to the evidence of the other witnesses. He would often mark the plan to indicate what had transpired and would not need to call me into the witness box. I suppose some of the plans which I drew are still in existence although I haven't seen one for years.

On one occasion whilst I was still attached there, I was required to appear in uniform for the Harrow and Eton cricket match at Lords. I had the task of shepherding them across the road, complete with boaters, top hats and their terribly important parents, or at least they appeared to be terribly important. While I was doing this task, I saw coming towards me down Avenue Road, a very well built young lady with a little boy on a tricycle pedalling along like mad in order to keep up with her. She approached me and asked me where my funny hat was, in a foreign accent. I told her that I was wearing it, indicating my helmet. She told me that she was going to have a picnic that afternoon and would I join them, so we made an arrangement for a rendezvous. At our meeting point I saw her walking toward me carrying a hamper, a large beach ball and a travelling rug, and her boy was still pedalling his little legs off. Once we settled down, she decided to remove her dress, being a very warm day, revealing a one piece bathing costume. She was so well endowed in her chest region that she had to also wear a bra to support it all. She turned out to be a Swiss au pair and came from Lucerne where her father had a grocery shop. We continued our relationship mainly because during one of our more intimate moments at the picnic she had whispered that she was going to 'kill me,' and well it was just too good a chance to let go. It can now be said that she had the biggest pair of breasts I have ever had the pleasure of fondling. She had a very nice hobby painting small flowers onto partially glazed crockery which she would then have refired. They were beautiful works of art.

The family she was living with went away for a fortnight to the south of France and so she had invited her parents to come and visit her for a week. I had a most enjoyable dinner party with them and supplied her dad with his favourite wine Château Neuf Du Pape, and gave flowers to her mother.

Dad was a member of the Swiss Alpine Club and his grocers shop was the biggest in Lucerne. Marie Louise was a very talented girl and a great conversationalist. We had a very pleasant relationship which ended when her married boyfriend from Switzerland appeared on the scene.

COMING UP THE FAST LANE

Once a year at Marylebone there was a day trip to the races, or to put it in other words six constables and a sergeant had to perform their duty. We were all taken by van to Victoria Station where we boarded the train, which also contained lots of other police. The railway porter came along and stuck reserve labels on the windows of the carriages we were in.

Our duties consisted of looking after a walkway across the five furlong spur that ran across the centre grounds of the main race track. It was not a difficult job as there was only one occasion during which the little bit of hallowed turf was used.

The sergeant in charge selected the constables he wanted with him: an old pre-war policeman who was knowledgeable about racing, and five other lads who got on well together. The sergeant informed the rest of us that we would need thirty shillings to enable bets to be made. The sergeant and an older PC selected the horses, another PC put the bets on with a nearby bookie and my job was to collect whatever winnings were due to us, if any. It was a lovely summer's day and we spent most of it drinking Bass bitter obtained from a nearby marquee. As far as the selection of runners in each race went we did reasonably well, and come the last race, a five furlong sprint down our very own track, we selected two horses and did a double bet. Off they went, and after about three furlongs our two horses were well in front, when suddenly the leading horse began to slow down. Slower and slower till the jockey dismounted just in time before the poor horse fell dead, right there and then from a ruptured blood vessel in its lungs. It was a rather sad end to a beautiful day, not only for the horse but for our wallets too.

THE FLUFF BALL

I was walking up Baker Street one night when a cab driver stopped me and told me that there were some men breaking into a tobacconist shop near Baker Street Underground Station. I walked at a fast pace to Marylebone Circus and crossed over onto St John's Wood ground and walked up the elevated roadway that ran along the front of the station. Not knowing the grounds as well as I should, I would have been better off staying on Marylebone Road, and approaching the villains from the other end near Madame Tussauds where I would have come upon them without forewarning. There were three of them. Two ran off on seeing me, and the third who was inside, behind the broken shop window handing stuff over, got out just a little after the other two. I gave chase up Allsop Place at the side of Madam Tussauds down Baker Street and into Melcome Street. I blew my whistle in an effort to get assistance, and being the first time to do so in three years of service, all I got was a mouthful of fluff. It dawned on me that I could be in trouble if the three of them had stopped to confront me. Then I noticed under a parked car, two little feet sticking out. He was quickly dragged out from his dismal hiding place and transported to Marylebone Lane by the very same taxi that had first warned me of the incident. The driver charged me 2/6d for the ride and had just been cruising around watching the whole chase and capture without even offering assistance, which puts him in the bracket of the tight-fisted armchair heroes of this world.

BETTERING JIM

I was walking down Harley Street, London's well known home of private medicine, on a beautiful summer's night, around the midnight hour when walking towards me came a gentleman who must have been an early forty-something, wearing a dinner jacket with a black bow tie. On each arm there was a gorgeous young lady, obviously twins, who were giggling merrily away. As they neared me I wished them a goodnight and cheekily said, 'You're a bit greedy sir, with two of them.' He happily replied, 'What do you think of them? They're my daughters, I've wined and dined them, taken them to the theatre, and they are bloody pests. Come and have a drink with us and see if you can keep them in order.'

Well how could I turn an offer like that down? I spent a very enjoyable hour with them all. The girls took it in turns to try my helmet on and were constantly teasing me. Dad was grateful for the break that I had given him and we had a great conversation about how the world was shaping up. I left and continued on my way.

Such incidents made life very worthwhile and in that manner I met many people and I believe that it helped me to better understand human nature. To this day I am convinced that there are people of great social standing and others of great wealth (it doesn't necessarily follow that the two go together) who would welcome an ordinary intelligent conversation with someone. All too often I've discovered that all types cling to their own sort and it further consolidates their narrowness of mind. They finish up with the most shocking case of tunnel vision.

Now of course, this is solely my opinion but you've got to ask yourself, who do you know of great wealth who talks of only money and little else? Take that away from them and they are quite shallow. It's in my books at least, as the Gucci Syndrome.

I have met policemen who could mend antique clocks, sing Bavarian hunting songs, make exquisite furniture and still wouldn't stand for any nonsense from anyone, irrespective of their standing. They were individuals who didn't conform; they were good at their jobs and had that certain way with them that was both reassuring and fascinating.

THE STAG PARTY

It's always a good thing to keep up morale; we worked hard, put in long hours and turned up for anything that we were called out to. So of course, rewards came with the job. Once a year our Annual Stag Party was arranged at Elliot House. This took place in the basement gymnasium with a scaffolding arrangement put up at the back to act as 'The Gods.'

The front row was nearly taken up by all the publicans and bookmakers with the senior officers amongst them. All the proceeds went to the Orphans' Fund. Most of the stars that appeared in the West End theatres were there to entertain us well into the early hours of the morning. They had been fetched and returned by police cars, which were also supplied with scotch for their pleasure.

The actor John Blythe who lived on the ground acted as MC and the Beverly Sisters, Edmundo Ross and Tommy Trinder were but a few of our special guests that came along to make the Annual Event extra special and a great success. I gather that in later years the event died a death due to the likelihood of allegations being made regarding the publicans and bookies there. All good things must come to an end.

BELOW THE KNEE

We occupied single rooms in the section house, with no locks on the doors. However, we discovered that if you were to drill a small hole through the bit that goes into the door jam, and put a one and a half inch oval nail through it the room was quite secure when one was entertaining. Our guests would be taken through the basement to avoid the front hall and the section house sergeant, and then up we would go in the lift to our floor. I often waited in the foyer for the lift and watched it go up with a very trim pair of ankles next to a pair of police boots.

Speaking of boots, that reminds me, I used to find that when I put my boots on before my trousers and then pulled my trousers up they gave a reasonably good shine to the toecaps of the boot. When you realized that your knees were dirty then it was time to go to the dry cleaners.

IN PRIVATE

A fire broke out at lunch-time in a mews cottage which was occupied by three outrageous queers, who managed to escape the blaze. The two Alsatian dogs that lived with them were the ones who had saved their lives by alerting them in time before the fire spread. Sadly the dogs did not survive the fire, and it was not a very pretty sight for me watching the three grown men cuddling one another.

In those days buggery was a crime; in fact it was thought to be an abominable crime with both sodomites and the catamites guilty.

Look at the members of parliament reducing the age of consent. Are we such a nation that we find that the parliamentary system is right, or are the members of that body so bent in their ideals that perversion is now the norm and that it is politically correct to allow people to do as they so please, as long as it's in the privacy of their own home, or at least a contained place of privacy?

The next step as I see it is the reduction of the age of consent of heterosexuals, so as to give some comfort to the paedophiles that now despoil our society, and quite a few have had the chance to do so as members of the elected house of parliament.

The number of men arrested importuning in the West End toilets had some famous actors, politicians and members of the legal profession among them.

Stan Bassham and I were taking two drunks to court one day who I had arrested for being disorderly. One of them was queer, and whilst in the van kept up a conversation with yours truly. He talked to me whilst I chose to ignore him. Stan made a comment saying, 'He fucking fancies you.' At the court after giving my evidence the magistrate asked the defendants if they wished to ask the officers any questions. The queer said, 'He's telling a pack of lies.' He was then fined thirty shilling for his cheek.

YOU'RE NICKED, MY SON

I was walking home from duty through Paddington's ground when I saw a man trying to open one of those free standing cigarette machines outside a shop. It was 11.30 p.m. and I arrested him and walked him to Paddington Green Police Station. As he was trying to open the machine I put that down to the fact that he was a little worse for the drink.

At the station I told the sergeant on duty that I had a drunk for someone and sat the rascal down in the charge room. He then stated that he had done a job in Walsall. I at once removed him from the charge room and took him to the CID office where I interrogated him, discovering that he had broken into a pub about a fortnight before. I telephoned the police station in Walsall and discovered that there was indeed a suspect wanted for such a crime. He was then transported to Walsall Police who came down to get him. He was still wearing the shoes that he had stolen from the pub when I arrested him. The bottle of gin he took had been consumed and the missing twenty-five pounds had been spent.

A week or so later I had to go to the magistrates' court there to give evidence as to his arrest for the committal proceedings. I was met at the bus station by a local detective sergeant who apologized on behalf of his governor who had wanted to meet me and welcome me to Walsall. I was told that I would meet him in the morning. I was taken to a hotel; I believe it was called the Priory Hotel.

The sergeant took me to the reception desk and asked for the manager, introducing me as Mr Goodwin from Scotland Yard. A great fuss was made over me and I was in turn introduced to three elderly gentlemen in the main bar of the hotel. I then spent the evening drinking treble scotches and smoking Passing Cloud cigarettes into the early hours, telling stories from the book 'Fabian of the Yard,' which had just been published. I also had to invent stories of my own to keep the evening going and to keep my listeners captivated. I must admit that I didn't feel too well in the morning and a large breakfast put in front of me proved too much to handle.

I was taken to meet the local superintendent and was thanked for my help. After giving my evidence I went back to his office where I was invited to help draft a letter of commendation to the commissioner in London, which I did later receive. The villain got two years inside as an incorrigible rogue.

THE EGG AND SPOON RACE

We held an annual sports day at Hendon, nothing too energetic, although one year I decided to enter almost every event and ended up winning about fifteen shillings. You got five bob for a win and nothing for a place.

They were great family days out; the children were kept well amused and fed with lots of ice cream.

I ended up being disqualified for running in the one mile walk and at the end of the day I was completely knackered.

The following year having already exhausted all the events from the previous year, I volunteered to be on duty and found myself covering the whole of the ground. There was a sergeant on duty at the station and his advice to me was to keep out of sight. Bear in mind this was a Sunday in the Fifties and very little ever happened then.

NO NONSENSE JOCK

When I was aid to CID on night duty, there would be two aids and a detective sergeant to cover the division and to deal with any serious crime. One of the sergeants was a Jock Forbes, who operated out of Paddington and most nights we would travel from there to Albany Street where we would be on call. We were on our way there from Paddington, travelling along the Harrow Road with Jock Forbes driving, when, as we were trotting along an Irishman shouted out, 'Fucking coppers.' So Jock stopped the car, got out, walked across the road and laid the Irishman out with one punch, got back into the car and as he began to drive off stated that he couldn't stand drunken Irishmen.

Jock Forbes went on to be in charge of all regional crime squads in the UK. He was of the old school and wouldn't stand for any nonsense from anyone.

WIZ AND 'OISTERS

I was in the CID office one day, just about to commence a tour of duty as aid to CID when Detective Inspector Wallace, 'Wal', came out of his office and suggested that we should patrol the big stores and be on the lookout for the whiz and 'oisters. Also in the office, was Inspector Bailey, a tall, charming man, who said to Wal, 'Oysters?'

'Yes, 'oisters,' Wal replied.

'Oh you mean h.o.i.s.t.e.r.s.' Literally spelling it out.

'Yes 'oisters,' replied Wal.

This was the age of slang, villains were known to be chummy and a conversation in-house at that time would not have been understood outside. Whiz meant describing a villain whizzing something out of someone's bag or pocket. Hence whiz and 'oisters: shoplifters.

A CASE OF THE BLUES

On the Marylebone Road opposite Madame Tussauds an old boy had been knocked down and killed by a bus. It happened at about 11 a.m. I had been only a few moments away and so was soon on the scene. I produced a sketch plan to go with my report and later prepared it for the inquest. The coroner went over the plan with me, and on this occasion I pointed out the spot were the man had put his walking stick against a low wall. The corner formed the opinion that he had in fact thrown himself under the bus and had not been knocked down accidentally.

THE PEST

The civilian typist in the CID office was a big girl who wore cheap perfume to hide a distinctly unpleasant body odour. She was a bloody pest as she always wanted to join in with every conversation my fellow officers would have. Invariably butting in when her opinion wasn't needed. It got to such a point that she was finally grabbed, bent over, her knickers pulled down and her arse stamped with one of the station stamps. She didn't pester us for a few days and then slowly regained her confidence and continued to remain a pest until the day I left Marylebone Lane. Nowadays of course such action wouldn't be tolerated and we would most definitely be severely dealt with.

WHO FARTED?

There were four of us travelling down Marylebone High Street one afternoon in the Morris J4 van with Shag Reece at the wheel, when someone farted. Shag suddenly stopped the van in the middle of the road, jumped out the car with the engine running and ran off down the street. We all sat there like lemons until he decided to return. He then just got back in and we drove to the station.

Part Three

Transfer to Deptford, Lewisham Train Crash

TRANSFER

During the time I served at Marylebone Lane I was married and had to move into married quarters on Formosa Street. The outcome of this was that I had a longer journey to work each day which was not a problem. The flat we occupied was in a large converted house and was leased to the police by a private landlord. The lease ran out and so we had to vacate the premises to the nearest available quarters, which incidentally were situated at Blackheath on Shooter's Hill Road. I travelled from there to Marylebone Lane each day, but for early turn I began to find the journey a bit of a drag. In the end I decided to ask for a transfer to the nearest station to my house, and finished up being posted to Deptford on 'M' Division.. Bearing in mind that I had served for the last seven years in the West End of London with the lifestyle that went along with it, finding myself at Deptford, the home of dockers, with the Surrey and Rotherhithe Docks close to hand, I found the change traumatic. I can say without fear of contradiction that I was not too happy to be posted there. Anyway, I made the best of what I thought was a bad job and knuckled down to the task.

OI! NO!

At the junction of New Cross Road and Lewisham Way there was the Harp Club, for the Irish in the neighbourhood. I was called out one evening to a fight that was going on in there. On entering I saw two men in the middle of the dance floor one astride the other; the one on top was knocking seven bells out of the one on the floor. Now in order to stop the pair of them from attacking me, which was quite likely to happen if I were to ask them politely to desist from fighting, I had developed the technique of tapping the one with the upper hand on the shoulder, and then as he looked around, thump him one hard in the ear. So this I did and it indeed gave the desired effect. The fighting stopped and the trouble-maker was thrown out of the Harp Club. The one I had clouted turned out to be the one that was trying to get rid of the other. I apologized and explained my way of doing things. He had no ill feelings and said, 'You pack a good punch, sir,' and so I ended up spending a couple of hours with the lad drinking draft Guinness and having lavish hospitality showered my way.

THE LEWISHAM TRAIN CRASH

The Lewisham train crash happened at 6 p.m. on December 4th 1957, at St Johns Station, three weeks before Christmas. Two commuter trains had collided. I had just walked into Deptford Police Station when the station sergeant sent everyone to the scene in the police van.

It was a foggy, damp, miserable evening which was actually the reason for the crash, as was later reported. I had just spent time on traffic control at New Cross Gate. When we reached the New Cross Road we saw that a fire engine from Kennington, also on the way to the scene was in some difficulty as to the direction of the accident. I volunteered to assist and stood on the nearside of the engine as it made its way under my direction. We had to veer from side to side of the road in order to keep in touch with the kerb. When we got to the scene, we could see that it was a major disaster; like nothing I had seen before. Below the embankment wall there were already bodies covered with blankets on stretchers. Up the embankment ladders had been placed to assist us to get to the trains involved.

At such a time as this we were always allowed to get on and do the best we could. I climbed up onto the first train and below I could see doctors treating a casualty that was trapped under the train. It was a young lady whose legs were being amputated and she was in fact the last victim of the crash who died, about two days later.

I must admit that when I reached the scene I couldn't see what all the fuss was about. It wasn't until I walked along the track towards the rear of the first train that I saw the magnitude of this terrible accident. The first train had been hit in the rear by another train, packed with commuters and the impact had caused the second train to whip and bring down a bridge support and the three hundred ton bridge with it, right onto the travelling train. It had in fact planed off one carriage top and had come to rest on another, compressing its original height of ten feet to about five. The people inside had been compressed. There were bottoms, hands and heads sticking out all grossly enlarged from the pressure. Various parts of the human anatomy were everywhere. I saw a small bone fixed to the end of a piece of angle iron. There was no trace of blood. Looking under the carriage there was a body towards the ground with its entrails hanging over its face. The fire brigade was attempting to move the bodies from this carriage. In order to move a group of morbid onlookers who were standing gawping in the car park to the rear of a block of flats close to the railway, I went down there and asked them to move. I had one silly sod tell me that he was a friend of the commissioner and so he wasn't going to budge. I told him in no uncertain manner that I didn't give a fuck who he knew and threatened him with arrest if he didn't move. There were quite a number of people there, really too many for me to manage alone, so I called for assistance and we shifted them out of the flat complex altogether and way up the road where we subsequently had a barrier erected.

In one of the rear coaches in a compartment which was festooned with corpses covered in blankets, we had a real old cockney woman who had one foot trapped but apart from that she was uninjured. The firemen were doing all they could to release her. The language of that girl was something to be heard. Apparently the foot they were dealing with was alright, it was her other one that was trapped by the debris.

Most of the policemen were picking up personnel possessions for safe keeping although one private individual was arrested for looting. I also assisted in removing some of the bodies for the waiting ambulances. Volunteers had been called for. The local station and Ladywell Baths next door to Lewisham Station had to be turned into a mortuary. I didn't envy them; their job was to assemble the various incomplete body parts that had been brought in. They developed a sort of gallows humour and had a thankless task.

After about three hours at the scene I needed a break and walked up the line for a quiet smoke only to find a charming Salvation Army lass there with her tea urn set up. All she said was, "Would you like a cup of tea, officer?" I always found the Salvation Army were there at such times like these when we needed them the most, and didn't ever impose themselves on you, which was a breath of fresh air. I had a cup of tea and a fag and then walked back to the scene ready to help in any way I could.

We were all trying to remove bodies and clear up the scene but it never seemed to end and it was not until about 3 a.m. that I decided to go home, having had enough. At the station I booked off and was asked if I would volunteer to go back the next day at about 2 p.m. So the next day I headed directly there, having booked on by phone.

One of the problems was the weight of the bridge bearing down on the wreckage. A firm had turned up to lift or to exert pressure where it was needed. It had a separate manual pump connected to the rams and could apparently move great weight. Whether or not it was used I'm not sure but it appeared to have great potential.

I helped to remove the last body from under the bridge who had had the full weight of it on his head. It was not a pretty sight and brought the whole incident for me to an unhappy conclusion. I am constantly reminded of that time by the various rail accidents that always happen to occur just before Christmas.

One has to consider the awfulness of having to inform the relatives and to realize the sadness of bereavement especially where there are children involved. I developed a way of informing relatives of the death of a loved one, which I like to think I did with great sympathy and understanding but one never got used to it. I came away from their homes feeling sad and shaken by the upset that had now hit their lives. Bodies were a different matter: one had to treat them with a little coldness and put out of your mind that they were someone's father, wife or child. It was an item that one had to dispose of in a methodical way and provided you followed the rules there was never any problem.

One also had to consider the enormity of writing a concise report of a major disaster, a task taken on by the local senior officer, to appreciate the work-load involved and to be aware that the civil action, which required one's attendance, may be years away. This was also the case when dealing with a road accident; you would receive a letter from a firm of solicitors asking you to attend some civil court to give evidence of something that had happened years before.

Marble Arch traffic during the smog, December 1952. Copyright The Daily Sketch.

President Kennedy and MacMillan, passing through Hammersmith Broadway. Copyright The Daily Express

Yours truly at Imber Court for the dress rehearsal for the Royal Show. Copyright Commissioner of the Police for the Metropolis.

Kosygin coming from Heathrow, passing over the Hammersmith flyover. Copyright The Daily Mirror.

Kosygin, Downing Street, man with goggles down is Ron Cross. Copyright The Daily Mirror.

Kodak Police Photographic Exhibition at Kodak House, Kingsway. Copyright of Kodak.

Having a discussion with an under secretary of the Home Office at the above exhibition. Copyright of Kodak.

Biggin Hill, the team of sixteen I trained for the Royal Agricultural Show at Stoneleigh Chief Inspector Baldwin on the extreme left. Copyright Commissioner of the Police for the metropolis.

R.A.I. Hall Amsterdam, Precision team lining up at the completion of the display. Copyright not known.

Forty Motorcyclists with their Triumph Motorcycles at the Triumph Factory at Meridenn. Route for the investiture of the Prince of Wales. Copyright the Triumph Motorcycle Company.

Publicity photo for Storno Radios in St. James's. Copyright Storno Radios.

Photograph of yours truly, December 1956, north side of Cavendish Square accompanied by back up for the Christmas Shopping with a P.C. from Holloway, the second with my Motorcycle prior to a display.

Part Four

Joining the Traffic Section. Training at the Hendon Driving School. Out and About: Accidents and Incidents. Manslaughter trial at Kingston Assizes. Personalities and others.

TRAFFIC PATROL

After about twelve months' service at Deptford Police Station, I thought that it was time for a change in my career. The career instructor was called for and I applied to join traffic patrol. I had seen them driving their cars and riding their motorcycles and thought that this style of life would suit me just fine. I managed to persuade the Selection Board that I was suitable material, and was posted to DT 8 at Lewisham.

I was sent post-haste to Hendon Driving School for a basic motorcycle course, although I had been riding a motorcycle for about three years. Nevertheless, I found the course exciting and the instruction first class. I had a Sergeant Newton as my instructor, and after a few days in the classroom we attempted to ride the Triumph Speed Twins on the internal roadway at the rear of the school. The following day we were out on the road. One novice would be in front with the instructor following him, with two more of us following behind.

One soon learnt that the rearward vision was essential if only in order to see that your fellow students were keeping up. When in front you were under the gaze of the instructor who would ride up alongside you to point out errors in your riding, also showing you the easy control he had over his machine. We gradually travelled further along and thoroughly enjoyed ourselves. We became more competent, our speed increased and the classroom lectures on the Hendon system of riding came to the fore.

I passed the course and returned to Lewisham. The next stage was to be taught to drive a car. To assist in this I was posted to Operational Cars for a four hour stint. The control of the vehicle, especially by the old courtesy cops, those that had been Traffic Patrol before the war was most enlightening.

I had never driven a car before I went to Hendon, and as a raw trainee driver I had a hard task passing the course on my final drive, which is the one when you are tested. I stalled the Hillman Minx about three times and although I passed I was invited to come back for a retest. At the garage I was put under the care of first class drivers who knocked me into shape.

Fred Blyes philosophy was that, 'When in doubt close your eyes and put your foot down.' I was now driving a Wolseley 6/80 and was subjected to the retest at the garage, which I passed.

After a few thousand miles of driving I was sent to Hendon for the intermediate car course, which once passed, would make me a fully operational car driver. The standard for this is equivalent to the Institute of Advanced Drivers' course. What the lads at Lewisham had taught me came to the fore and I passed yet another test, this one for best driver and best student. To pass the latter one I had to know the Highway Code inside and out and the Road Craft Manual in the same way. I attended various other advanced Traffic

Patrol courses which dealt mainly with vehicle examinations and accident investigations. I finished up with a pass on the advanced driving course, and came out as the best driver and best student again, but missed the skidding top position through hitting one cone on the test.

On the advanced course my instructor's name was Ginger Ellis, also known as Nutty Ellis because he loved Cabury's Whole Nut chocolate. The three students clubbed together and got a bar of Whole Nut chocolate that would keep him sweet for the rest of the day.

By this time we were using Wolseley 6/90s and over the years we had Jaguars. When I finished at the garage we were driving Rovers. I should explain that on the advanced car course we were given different cars to drive each day and you had to drive them fast and safely.

The set up for the course was that three students would be assigned to an instructor in a car, and another car containing the same number would be linked to us for the sequence of events that followed; the car in front as the bandit car, and the car behind as the police car. The first day on the road I was driving the bandit car, setting off at a fast pace, followed by the other car. We had stopped off for our morning tea break somewhere in Hertfordshire and had been there for some minutes before the other car turned up. After a discussion, the instructors decided that I was too fast and I only drove from then on for the rest of the course in the following car.

I enjoyed the challenge of each different vehicle and found all that I had been taught previously slotted right into place. At long last I found something that I loved and was good at.

THE COMMENTARY

We had to develop the technique of giving a commentary while driving along. This would last for about twenty minutes out of the forty minutes that you spent behind the wheel. It was as if you were being programmed like a computer and enabled a good style of driving, based on road craft being developed.

There were only two of us from Traffic Patrol on the course, the others were all divisional.

During my time at the driving school I stayed in lodgings that had been arranged through the school. They were mainly widows who welcomed the income, and the company.

On the advanced course, my landlady supplied the finest packed lunch, which we had to take with us on our long drives. The instructors knew of her yummy treats and would hover about as I unpacked the goodies.

There were of course other fringe benefits, the main one for me being that I could take a leisurely walk to school after breakfast, whilst it took the other students a couple of hours to get to and from their homes. At the end of the day I could amble my way back to my lodgings, take a nice bath or shower, have my dinner and then settle down to study the books that were essential.

The final drive for the advanced course consisted of two parts. First getting into the car and adjusting the seat and mirrors, and then driving off under the direction of the chief superintendent; being allowed about five minutes to settle down and get used to the vehicle. He would then tell us that we had just received an emergency call and off we would go. I would have to give the commentary all the time and after about ten minutes he would then tell you to stop the commentary and resume at a normal speed. After a few minutes he would give information about a car: its colour, make and registration and then tell you to chase it. I was fortunate to see the car coming up behind me and accelerated when he finally over took me, and so the chase began. The bandit car would not give an indication of where he was going or when he would make a turn. I would have to keep the commentary going all the time. The chase lasted about ten minutes or so, through heavy arterial traffic and country lanes. Finally I was told that it was enough and then drove back to the starting point so that the next candidate could go. That afternoon the results were given and the comments were passed out. The driver of the bandit car was Noddy Newton, who had been my instructor on the basic motor cycle course and who went on to be in charge of the whole driving school.

INSPECTION DAY

Wednesday at the driving school was inspection day. The chief superintendent would walk through the varied ranks of the motorcyclists, basic, intermediate, and advanced drivers; inspecting their general smartness. The Traffic Patrol people had to see that we had the wire in our hats to keep the shape. Normally we would remove them to give a more rakish appearance. One wag had the governor stop to remove a small piece of cotton on his serge jacket. He pulled and pulled and still it came, until he had a giant spool of it. The young rascal had only gone and rigged the whole thing up by having a spool of cotton in his pocket, through which he had carefully threaded a small piece sticking out of his sleeve, and finished up getting a right bollocking.

That was the last time any more pieces of cotton or fluff were touched during the inspections by the chief superintendent. Unlike the story of the rat that would keep returning back down that same passage looking for the cheese, our superintendent wasn't that rat.

Most careers were ruined in the gents' toilets. One of the lads would be going on about how they really felt about a particular instructor or inspector, only to find out later that he had been sitting in one of the cubicles listening to every last word, and had their card marked for the rest of the course.

ON THE ROAD

The change from foot duty to traffic is quite a big step, as I found out. Being on foot enables you to be in close contact with the people around you. You are also available at a moment's notice to react to whatever circumstances happen to arise. On a motorcycle or in a car there is no such contact and you only get to deal with the things that happen with other moving vehicles and so very seldom did dealing with a pedestrian ever come up.

Initially as a new Traffic Patrol during the winter you rode the motorcycles and in the summer you drove the cars. The older chaps did the reverse. Age sometimes has its privileges.

We didn't have radios on the bikes and so we would just disappear onto the grounds for eight hours and enforce the traffic law, to try and keep the average car driver from killing himself and, more importantly, others.

I met many motorists who would proudly boast that they had never had an accident, but they never seemed to mention how many they had caused.

Accidents were the main job of the cars and we were called to the more serious ones when the foot duty police needed our expertise. Some of the drivers were reluctant to deal with accidents.

One particular chap that if you were ever in the car with, would in fact slow down on receiving a 999 call. He was an idle bastard and seldom put pen to paper. Nothing would get him to work and I was amazed that he managed to get to retirement without being found out.

My partner and I would take four hours driving at a time. Most of it was fast driving although between calls we would just cruise around or be laid up in some side street. Some days were quite boring, just driving around, yet other days were full of accidents and incidents to deal with.

It was quite remarkable to follow a car for about half a mile at a speed well in excess of the speed limit, without being spotted by the car driver. I took the view that if they were driving at such speed and got caught then they deserved to be reported. That was also the case if I had stopped someone to give them a bollocking about something or other that was dangerous, and they argued the case. I thought the best place to argue would be before a magistrate. If the telling-off was accepted, we always parted on good terms. I tried to impress upon them that I didn't want them to have an accident and kill themselves, or anyone else for that matter. If you could get it across to them that they could be a victim of their own stupidity and do harm to their own passengers, they did begin to take note.

One of my colleagues stopped a car to tell the driver that his rear door was on the half catch. He got off of his motorcycle to speak with the driver and closed the door properly for him. He was also concerned as the gentleman driving the car had children with him, and had the car been hit the children could have been thrown out into the road. A passing motorist stopped his car and called out to the driver, 'You weren't speeding,' to which the other gentleman replied, 'Why don't you mind your own business.'

We did try to help the general public but some persisted in being silly buggers and were beyond help. They were applicants for the Ramblers Club of Great Britain and would finish up being disqualified and forced to walk.

THE GOAT THAT STOLE THE FISH

Taffy Williams, alias Ron, or 'The Goat,' came from Brecon and also played bowls, mainly with the chief superintendent, and was often heard to say, 'Good wood, sir.' He was a great motorcyclist and was one of the original members of the Precision Team and Escort Groups. His only downfall was that he was lost if he ever left a bus route. When the Goat was accepted as a Flying Squad driver his knowledge of navigating away from the bus routes came to the fore.

He had relatives in Brecon and one of his cousins farmed there, with whom I had the pleasure of meeting on two occasions. The Goat whilst on holiday there was caught taking fish by unlawful means and was fined the handsome sum of two pounds. He had been tickling trout and numerous fish were found in the boot of his car.

Now the naughty thing was that the Goat stood the risk of being sacked as a policeman for such a crime, and in consequence he had to appeal. We all ended up chipping in half a crown, and off went the Goat together with Isabel, his Scottish wife, and the children to Brecon, where the appeal was being held. The Goat was in serious trouble until someone pointed out to the powers that be that the offence was one of a technical piscatorial nature and was not therefore a crime. In consequence the whole matter sank without trace, and the appeal was dismissed.

I'm convinced that the Goat and his family ended up having a nice holiday on the strength of the whip-round we had made for him. He used to live, or maybe he still does, in West Wickham. A widow lived next door to him, and had asked the Goat if he would decorate her lounge. He agreed, and asked me to assist. I was to make a whopping three pounds. So on my day off we both got stuck into the task at hand. I rubbed down the paintwork with sand paper, and the Goat followed on with the undercoat. I then followed on with the gloss and in about two hours the paintwork was done. The lady of the house had selected a very nice regency striped wallpaper with the predominant colour being rose. After a discussion, it was agreed that I would paste the paper and the Goat said he would hang it as he had more experience at it than me. We started off by the door and duly finished up on the other side of the door frame, the paper with its tell-tale stripe defiantly leaning about an inch or two off the vertical. The sad end to this tale is that the widow woman died about three months after we had decorated her room. I put it down to the fact that she walked with a lean due to the paper being out of true and that one day she leaned too far, fell over, and died.

Now the Goat's retired and in his spare time as a bailiff likes to evict young mothers with their infants onto the streets; in between that and the bowls, he's never around.

At DT8 we had many policemen that had joined before the war, a great number had served in the forces and among them was Reg Perrington who was with the Airborne Troops that landed on D-day. I always thought that he looked a bit like Sir Edmund Hillary of Everest fame. He lived off Hayes Lane in Bromley and he referred to where he lived as Half a Kipper Land, because most people had large mortgages and could only afford half a kipper. Not strictly true but that's how he put it.

In those days quite a few wives stayed at home being good housewives. Their husbands were away at work and came home from their labours too tired to take the dog for a walk. Reg worked on the principle that if you wanted to meet the neglected young housewives, the essential thing was to acquire a hound yourself and then take it for walks. We all know that dogs on meeting each other have a good sniff round, especially the genital region, thus one was enabled to get into casual polite conversation with the aforementioned young wives. What developed from that was up to you. Reg had a nickname, 'Donkey Dick'. I formed my own conclusion that it must have been some large impedimenta that I gather he put to good use.

Sadly he died of a brain tumour before he came to his retirement age. He was a lovely person to know and a very competent policeman and a fantastic driver. At his funeral the church was jam-packed and he was sadly missed and mourned, no doubt, by many female dog owners.

DOWN TO THE CORE

One character that comes to mind is Dicky Craggs,

who had something like the style of David Niven. He was always full of the joys of living and was a good policeman. His forte was practical jokes which can only best be described in the following manner.

The Goat had a delicate stomach, he hated all foods that were not of the basic sort; egg, sausage and chips he liked, anything else he loathed. It was in the canteen when we were on early turn that the Goat had prepared himself the meal as above. We all sat down with him and as he started to consume his well fried meal, Dicky started to pull something from his nostril. The Goat looked up, and without a blink of an the eye ran from the canteen. Dicky had secretly put a length of bacon rind up his nose and down into the back of his throat waiting patiently for the right time to prank the Goat, whilst having a hard time keeping the tears back from his eyes. This was undoubtedly the most off-putting sight I had ever seen while someone was eating. When the Goat returned he found that his breakfast had been eaten by the others who were sitting at the table trying to hold themselves back from keeling over in fits of laughter.

This also happened to another one of the lads, Lofty Lay, who was called to the phone leaving an apple on his plate, and on his return only a core remained.

STINKY PANTS

I know many people are allergic to many things in life, foods, animals, medicines, but I never would have thought soap and water was one of them. We had a motorcyclist from TDM who had been involved in an accident whilst on duty. He was conveyed to the nearest hospital for immediate treatment. When the nursing staff removed his uniform and underclothes they found that he was covered in filth and obviously had an aversion to cleaning himself. The hospital was so shocked by what they had found that the garage superintendent was informed and went to the hospital to see the state of the filthy man with his own eyes. I never found out who he was but I know for a fact that he would have received the biggest bollocking of his life or anyone else's for that matter. What he smelt like is not hard to imagine; the fact that his wife even put up with him beggars belief.

WHAT CINEMA?

The first specially prepared accident car was a three litre Humber Super Snipe Estate, with a three gear column change. All the equipment was spread over the back of the vehicle and rattled around continuously. We had all the equipment that was thought to be needed at the scene of a serious accident. In consequence when posted to the car this was the thing that you dealt with.

I was on night duty with Bill Golley during the winter and the first call we had was a car that had crashed into a wall in Wandsworth. There was no other vehicle involved and the driver wasn't injured but we had to hang about until the vehicle was removed. In those days the police were responsible for the safe custody of the vehicle until it left the scene.

The weather was that sort of London drizzle that makes everything wet and I mean everything, even the inside of the car had that horrible damp feeling.

We then received a call to Charing Cross Road where a Chinese woman had been hit and run over by a car and had died. We attended the scene and reported the accident. At Charing Cross Hospital we were shown the body. We wrote up the report of the fatality and were once more on our way.

We were driving around Trafalgar Square when an accident that we had heard while on our way to the last incident, was asking for the duty officer to attend, which had now been reported to be a fatal accident. We volunteered and our assistance was readily accepted. The accident had taken place at Acre Lane near the junction with Denmark Hill. The driver of a Morris 1100 saloon had driven his vehicle into the rear of the cinema building and he was still trapped inside. The cinema hadn't suffered any damage but the car had, as had the driver who was still in the driver's seat. His head was well back and his face a deathly white with both eye sockets filled with congealed blood, with more blood coming from his mouth and from a wound on his left cheek. The ambulance was standing by and the fire brigade was all over the car, but for some reason they couldn't get him out. I examined the alleged corpse and found that he was trapped by the welts of his shoes which were caught under the pedals. I also discovered that he was actually unconscious through being dead drink.

Bill Golley always acted like a very efficient nursing sister in these circumstances and handed me some sterilized dressing which I put on the man's wounds. I then had the stretcher from the ambulance brought right up to the car. I lay down next to the driver with my head down by his feet and by applying pressure was able to bend the pedals away from his shoes, thus freeing his feet. I then applied triangular bandages to his angles, knees and thighs and, with the assistance of the ambulance crew, Sister Bill had the victim supported while I broke the back of the seat down in order for us to gently slide him out through the back car door and onto the stretcher.

He was taken to King's College Hospital which was only two hundred yard away. We hung around the scene for another twenty minutes and then headed back to the hospital where we found the man sitting up in the causality, arguing with the staff, and clearly drunk.

What had happened was that he had lost control of the vehicle after one too many and had crashed into the wall of the cinema and sustained five small wounds on his left cheek which had been caused from the shattered glass from the windscreen. Being in a complete paralytic state he had collapsed with his head back and the blood then ran into his eye sockets where it congealed. This was one of those occasions where not enough attention had been given to the casualty and a thorough examination had not been done. While he did look deceased a sensible examination would have shown otherwise. We had a lot to write about that night, and a late meal.

We were called to Southend Lane on Catford's ground where a young girl of about eight years old had been knocked off her bicycle and had sustained a ruptured calf muscle with a wound about four inches long and an inch wide. Her mother was at the scene and the crowd was just standing around doing nothing for the poor child. The mother told me that someone had said it was best to just let her bleed. Bill handed me the dressing and I bound up the wound which reassured both the mother and the girl. We called through to CO to ask them to let Lewisham Hospital know that there was a young girl on her way in and to tell them the nature of the her injury. She was taken there by ambulance and we followed on a few moments later having taken details of the car driver.

In casualty the young lady had been stripped down to her panties and when the doctor said they would have to be cut off her too the young girl burst into tears, telling the doctor that they were her best knickers. Mum and dad arrived shortly afterwards and dad was the most upset. The mother, who was an Irish lady, stated that she didn't know policeman did first aid. She gave me a pound note as a thank you for my help and suggested I buy myself a drink. I accepted the pound but didn't get myself that drink I instead had some flowers delivered to her for being a very brave little girl.

I find it strange that the reaction of parents to the injury or death of a child varies so much between the sexes. At the time either one or the other is upset and in tears and the other looks at the practicalities of the accident; there was never the time when both would be in tears. I suppose that as parents the practical one at that time had to look after the distraught one. That may be the explanation, I don't know but it could be worth a study.

The young girl, I later found out, was due to have a ballet examination shortly after but I never found out whether she had to give it up all together or just for a while.

A NICE CUP OF TEA, OR THREE

It was late turn with Ron Cross in the car when we were called to an accident in Balham in one of the back residential streets. Whilst we were dealing with the situation, a lady came out of a house nearby and asked if we would like to come in for a cup of tea when we had finished. Ron had taken the car to take particulars from one of the persons injured in the accident at Balham General Hospital. When he returned I had all the details necessary to complete the report so consequently knocked on the lady's door and said we had come for that cup of tea. We were invited in and enjoyed a pleasant ten minutes with her. When we left the lady's house another lady came up to us and said, 'When are you going to come and have that cup of tea?' Then it dawned on me that I had gone to the wrong house for the first cup. Obviously I hadn't been paying attention when she had first asked and hadn't noticed where she lived. It ended up happily and I apologized to the lady who had suddenly been confronted by two policemen asking her for a cup of tea. I explained what had happened and she saw the funny side of it and said that it had been nice having our company if only for a short while.

MUM?

A young lad who owned a 1934/5 Morris Eight Coupe had developed a technique whereby he could fly the door open as he was driving along due to the flexing of the chassis. He would put his brakes on hard, causing the door to swing shut. These were the days of the rear hinged, front opening doors. This worked very well until we were called one day to an accident where this young man was taking his mother for a ride. As he was driving down Annerley Hill he put his brakes on hard to close the door which had swung open. He was a few hundred yards on when he realized that his mother should have still been sat next to him and wasn't. Mum had fallen out of the car when the door flew open and had broken her arm. I tell you, I would like to have been a fly on the wall when they finally got home. I should think he'd be more careful next time whenever mum's around; that is if she ever decided to get back in that car with him again.

ONE LUCKY PUP

Bill Golley and I were called to an accident that had taken place in Plumstead. It involved a young girl of about eight years old, her puppy who was about eight weeks old and a young man driving his Mini. The young pup although on a lead, leapt into the path of the Mini and got itself wrapped around the front nearside suspension. The poor little girl was in tears as the puppy was still caught up in between the upper and lower front wishbones. With the driver's permission we jacked his car up, removed the wheel and unwrapped the dog which had been miraculously unharmed. I gave the little girl her puppy back who was now crying tears of joy. I asked the driver if he was happy with the result. He concurred, and the accident was never put on paper. I just couldn't see the sense of subjecting the little girl to such things as having to take her home to ask her details with either one or both of her parents present. She had her nasty turn and I was pleased to say that she and her puppy went off very happily.

One night, Ron Cross and yours truly were posted to the SETAC (Specially Equipped Traffic Accident Car) car in the Vauxhall area when a call came, in the early hours of the morning, asking for assistance at the scene of a serious accident in Epsom. The local traffic car wasn't available for whatever reason and as we didn't have a lot to do we took the call and set out for the wild neck of the woods. Ron navigated with the aid of the A to Z, while I drove. We finally arrived at the scene but couldn't see any sign of an accident. We drove on and turned round to have another look and discovered that the vehicle involved, an E-type Jaguar which we had been looking for in the street, was in fact upside down in somebody's front garden. It had demolished a three foot wall, together with the wooden fence that rested on top of it. It had then overturned onto the driveway of the house and slid along, finally coming to a stop in the flowerbed. There were numerous tyre marks on the roadway, the curb, the grass verge and the tarmacadam footpath, before it had shot up the bank hitting the wall. We discovered from the foot duty PC that the two people in the car had already been taken to hospital, together with a pedestrian who had been hit by the car as it careered off the road. The shoes of the poor chap who'd been hit were about fifty yards apart with one on the pavement and the other some way down the road.

As these gave some clue to the speed of the vehicle and the force of the impact, I asked that the shoes be left where they were so that we could have them included in a photograph of the scene.

We went to Epsom General Hospital were we found the people from the car not too seriously hurt. The pedestrian, John Hamilton Perry, aged twenty, the only son of a bank manager from Caterham, was in intensive care and was obviously dying. The local area car soon arrived with the father, who had the awful task of identifying his son to me. The lad's eyes were standing out completely black. His breathing was stertorous, and he had suffered severe brain damage. The local foot duty sergeant was there and I requested that we obtain statements, in detail, from people that were in the car and were present at the hospital, before they had time to put their heads together (i.e. collude and manufacture a story). The sergeant declined my request and said he would obtain statements later that day. I believe that was one mistake that could and should have been avoided, as the absence of a statement made soon after the accident would have cleared up a lot of complications that came to light later on.

Mr X the owner of the Jaguar, although shaken by the accident, complained only to me that he had a pain in his chest. His girlfriend, Miss X, told me that she had been driving and couldn't really remember what had happened. She told me she had seen the man, hit the brakes and skidded.

I returned to the scene of the accident later that day around about 3.45 p.m. and took more particular measurements and discovered that the marks made by the car extended in total, over a distance of 287 feet and consisted of skid marks, scrub marks and other tyre marks. There were five gouged rim marks on the curb edge made by the wheel rims and sump of the car. Such had been the speed that the car depressed the tyres on hitting the curb and the car rims had left these marks. There were also fan-shaped marks in the road where, as the car went out of control and swung to the left, it had momentarily left the road surface, coming down heavily at a different angle, causing the tyres to balloon out to give the fan shape, that is triangular marks. There were lamp posts that were near the scene and were on the same side of the road. I discovered that by driving the police car at speeds of up to eighty miles per hour, I could stop well before the second lamp post, having started to brake from the first one.

I was able to say with certainty that the speed of the Jaguar must have been in excess of eighty miles per hour. Having stuck my neck out on this point, I then had to attend the inquest where the result was that Miss X was committed for trial on a Coroner's Inquisition for manslaughter. The committal proceedings took place at the local magistrates' court where I had one hour and forty minutes in the witness box, answering question from the defence counsel, mainly about the speed of the Jaguar.

I mentioned kinetic energy, heat build-up, wheel loss and many other things which seemed to satisfy the court, but not the defence. I stated, in answer to his question that the minimum speed was not below fifty miles an hour. Back came the question, 'Could it have been going fifty-one miles per hour?'

'No, I am saying that it was not doing less than fifty miles per hour.'

So it went on and on like this for a while with the defence junior taking notes on everything I said. I was called up again as the last witness at the trial at the Kingston Assizes for the prosecution and found my way to the witness box.

I always found myself short of breath right at that point and it was only when I got into my stride that I found I could relax and welcome the challenge of the advocates' questioning.

Keeping in mind that what I was doing, thinking of myself as a representative of the general public for a monthly salary, while the barristers who were doing it for a fee, I always felt 'right' was on my side. I had nothing to gain and nothing to lose in being honest, except of course, my own peace of mind.

So the defence counsel stood up, looked at me and smiled and then looked at the judge and said, 'This man is an expert in his field and with your permission I'd like to ask him matters of opinion.' The judge nodded his head in approval, and then I was being asked for my opinion.

'I'm not going to ask you any more questions as to the speed of the vehicle, I accept that it was travelling at a fast speed, but I would however like to know the route over which it travelled before the accident took place.'

I mentioned that I didn't know. He then outlined the time that the Jaguar had taken to travel the ten miles from the drinking place, to the scene of the accident which was forty minutes, and asked me to give an estimate of the speed it would have required to cover that distance over that period of time. I now had to do some mental arithmetic and come up with the answer.

'Fifteen miles per hour,' I told him, to which his response was, 'This would be a slow speed for such a vehicle.'

'Painfully so,' I responded.

'Then could we assume that the vehicle had stopped?'

The defence's case was that the girl accused of manslaughter had not in fact been driving the vehicle at the time of the accident. Although she had steadfastly maintained that she was the driver, the defence was to bring in the argument that she was in fact suffering from retrograde amnesia. To support this argument they had employed the services of Professor Francis Camps, the Home Office Pathologist, whom I had first met at the incident with the queer who had hanged himself on that beautiful summer day. Camps gave evidence for about fifteen minutes on the subject. Quite honestly I didn't understand much of what he said.

Later, outside the court I asked the Professor whether or not the points he put to the court could not have given a different conclusion. To which he replied, 'Yes, but they are not paying me three hundred pounds.'

Through the years I developed a relationship with the Professor over the many postmortems of sudden deaths in which I was involved. I often watched him perform postmortem examinations because of my interest in first aid, whilst he gave me a running commentary on what he was looking for, and what he had found, which I was most interested in learning.

The outcome of the case of the Jaguar, with the jury failing to agree, the judge had no other option than to order a new trial.

During an adjournment I was asked by the second trial prosecution counsel if I was prepared to give evidence on behalf of the defence. I stated that if he, the Crown Prosecutor, representing the Director of Public Prosecutions had no objections, then I would be pleased to do so. There was a legal chat on these lines, and hence I had the unique experience of being called both by the prosecution and the defence.

The people owning the house where the car had come to rest had been the first on the scene, and the wife there stated in the second trial that she had seen the man get out of the car first. Bearing in mind that the car was upside down with a gap of only about nine inches between the top of the door and the ground, with the driver's side towards the witness, I was asked by the judge if in fact the passenger could have got out of the car first. I told him that as the passenger would have to get over the transmission tunnel, the gear level, the hand brake, the steering wheel and pass the driver in situ, albeit upside down, I thought it unlikely. I was asked by the judge if I was prepared to put it a little more strongly: I said that it would have been impossible.

Miss X was found not guilty, and outside the court room I was thanked by everyone concerned.

The owner of the piece got his comeuppance a little later when he was imprisoned for eighteen months for misappropriating clients' money. The coroner had asked Miss X to go out of the court before she had started to give her evidence at the inquest, so that she could have words with her solicitor about the meaning of the 'oath,' suggesting that we all knew she was being less than frank by stating that she was driving. But there it is, she stuck to her story and the real villain got off scot-free.

Sadly the only son of the bank manager died. I called in on him after the trail to pay my respects over a nice cup of tea. Thus was the case of the Jaguar in the garden.

A young Traffic Patrol was sitting on his motorcycle at a roundabout on Western Avenue having a breather, when he was suddenly confronted by an articulated lorry carrying pallets containing back axle assemblies for the BMC. They then overturned whilst negotiating the roundabout, crushing the young policeman. Over the radio I heard the call about the accident and I immediately volunteered to go. I was actually in the south of London at the time, but Oscar Control accepted my assistance and was thankful for my presence.

On my arrival at the scene the fire service were standing by as the policemen on duty were removing the heavy back axles and pallets off the motorcyclist. Once the objects had been removed enough so that the officer's jacket was visible, the lady doctor present cut his jacket and applied her stethoscope and declared that there was no sign of life. With nothing else we could do for this unfortunate man we stood back and let the fire service remove the rest of the fatal load. Tom Couchman was the superintendent from the now deceased officer's garage, who now had the unsavoury task of having to tell the wife of this terrible incident.

WHAT WALL?

A motorcycle combination coming away from the Crystal Palace race track had run out of road coming down hill and had collided with a garden wall. The rider was alright but when we arrived on the scene the sidecar passenger was unconscious and trapped in the sidecar. I examined the casualty and discovered that his neck was swollen and I suspected that it had been broken. I had my partner hold it still while I examined the rest of him and found out why he was trapped. I found that his feet had been caught up in the old tools and rubbish which had been allowed to accumulate in the sidecar and further aggravated by the sidecar body being dented onto his feet.

The fire brigade turned up and one of the firemen dropped a hydraulic jack on the legs of the casualty. I took hold of it and threw it in the road. I explained in the nicest way I knew how, that I would fully appreciate them keeping away due to the nature of the injuries. By removing his shoes we were able to place him on the stretcher keeping his spine in the same position that we had found him in. His head was held steady with little sandbags and he was conveyed to King's College Hospital at Denmark Hill, where about twenty minutes later he regained consciousness. The casualty officer said that if it had not been for the proper care taken at the scene of the accident he would have died from his injuries.

Now I'm not knocking the fire brigade on the whole as I know what kind of job they have on hand and what a great deal of risk is involved with it, but on three occasions I had reason to think that they had their priorities around the wrong way. The one incident I have just mentioned, the car in the cinema wall, and in the one to follow.

It was in Brixton when a dormobile van containing market traders dealing in cosmetics had braked suddenly. The sliding door which had been open slid shut under the deceleration braking and trapped the arm of the driver's father. When the fire brigade arrived they started to move the door forward to help the injured man and I was told to fuck off by the leading fireman. When the door was finally removed the man's broken arm fell to his side as they lifted him onto the pavement where I then applied first aid.

I had a word with the leading fireman and asked him what the idea of the exercise was. He told me, to remove the door. I pointed out that it was to free the man's arm and that the swinging of the arm down would have further damaged the arm, with the sharp ends of the broken bones cutting other tissues. I further pointed out that the next time he told a policeman to fuck off he would be arrested and that it would give me great pleasure in doing so. They did a good and brave job but I felt at times that they should have placed the comfort of the casualties first and not the exercise in the demolition of a car.

FIRST AID

One thing that all police had to do was to perform first aid to the injured. This started off with basic training and a refresher course every two years, together with a practical examination being compulsory. However, once you had joined Traffic Patrol at District Transport 8, more often than not you had to deal with injuries. I found that if I got stuck into what I had been taught the injured person would benefit. I had no small satisfaction in doing what I was trained to do before the ambulance arrived. I took such an interest in first aid that I joined the 'P' Division First Aid team, and we trained every Wednesday at Catford Police Station. Whether on or off duty I attended these training and practical sessions.

Stan Aylott was the Premier First Aid Officer and led the team. We took part in many competitions organized by the St John Ambulance Brigade and the Casualty Union, which was a separate organization that specialized in making the injuries look real. We, as a team, won many competitions and it became a very worthwhile exercise as I came across many injuries on a regular basis.

The 'P' Division team won the Grand Priors Competition in first aid organised on a yearly basis by the St John's people and included teams from all over the country.

Miners teams were exceptionally good. To enter one had to have reached a very high standard, and it was mostly those that in their working hours were called upon to do the practical application of first aid that flourished.

One of the things laid down in the St. John's First Aid Manual was that when securing a broken limb like an arm, adequate padding had to be placed between the injury and the trunk, in this case an arm, or between the legs if a lower limb was involved. There was no adequate padding supplied, and you were not allowed to use your own clothing, so I set out to find a solution for this problem.

In Lewisham there was a factory that manufactured plastic items, among which were the thin plastic bags to cover umbrellas. I acquired some of these bags for my first experiment. I firstly opened the neck and partially filled it with air and then secured the top with a knot. I then sat on it for my eight hour tour of duty and found that the air was still contained. Now if this was placed between the legs, say when the legs were secured by triangular bandages at the ankle, knees and thighs, the trapped air would move into the natural hollows of the limbs, above the ankles below and above the knees and at the top of thighs. The air was not compressed but merely trapped. In consequence the two limbs, that is the injured and uninjured felt as one, and when the casualty was moved, any shock to the injured limb was now cushioned, and discomfort for the casualty was greatly reduced. I did a full report on this idea and submitted it to the commissioner's office. Being somewhat naïve about such matters I failed to patent the idea. An inspector rang me up to ask if it was my own idea, and said that it being implemented. A few days later someone called to say that a first aider at Brixton said it was dangerous if used in the wrong hands and so the idea fell by the wayside. A few months later I received a Commissioner's Commendation for the idea.

I became the Traffic Division First Aid Secretary and set about organising annual competitions between the eight garages. We finished up with about five teams entering. The competition was a team effort and with the aid of various people I set up a scenario which could be reacted to with the circumstances shown, and if they were competent, conducted their examinations well and had trained hard could win brownie points; if they hadn't, well then they would lose them.

The casualties had been made up to show various injuries, some of them quite gruesome. The casualty volunteers had to act the part in every respect. In order for me to find a female casualty, I had to put in a request to the senior woman police officer for a volunteer to be found for me. I gratefully found a volunteer, and firstly had to explain to her that any examinations would be being made at skin level. It had to be done this way because in reality you could only find signs and symptoms that would come to light at skin level. Now for modesty sake, I asked that they were to wear bikinis under their bra and panties. The teams were made aware of this and were told in no uncertain terms what they could, and most certainly couldn't do.

I am proud to say that in my career as a policeman I have saved two lives and one leg. I'd like to further explain that the saving of these two lives was not a great demanding exercise. The most important thing in both cases was seeing that the spine was kept in the right position, and of course some traction had to be applied while being removed from the wreckage and from the wreckage to the stretcher and from the stretcher to the ambulance.

There were many times when sensible practice of first aid ensured that the condition was not worsened and no further aggravation caused. At that time first aid was a unique treatment for a casualty. Many doctors back then were at a loss as to what to do without the necessary equipment and the right kind of help. So much so that it came down to our own men, Stan Aylott and two others of the P Division team, going to Guy's Hospital to give a lecture on first aid to the student doctors.

One of the accidents I had to deal with was in

Blackheath. An old man had been knocked down by a car, and three doctors from a surgery near by lifted him out of the road and onto the pavement. When I arrived they asked me if I could find out where the bleeding was coming from. It turned out that the man was bleeding from the rectum and through the doctors having moved him off the road his fractured pelvis had cut through an artery causing the bleeding. The sad thing was that he and his wife were Jehovah's Witnesses and because of this the man refused a blood transfusion and in consequence died the next day.

The point I am trying to get across here, is that the practical side of first aid is the life saver, not the theory, or assumed knowledge at that very single moment in time. You should understand by now that you do not move people who are injured, unless of course if it's very minor. As far as traffic is concerned, the traffic can wait all day until the injured person is safely moved into the ambulance, and then off to hospital.

We must remember that somebody's life, future and future well-being are far more important than you missing your connecting flight.

Remember it could be you out there lying on the road and so I'm sure you can appreciate having to take a break from your busy life, in order to save another's.

PATHOLOGY

In Cyprus during the struggle for independence from the British an unarmed British soldier, a sergeant, was shot in the back in Famagusta. He was accompanied by his small son of three years and I will always remember the picture in one of the daily papers of the man lying dead with his infant child crying his eyes out. The EOKA terrorist responsible was arrested and charged with murder. However at his trial the pathologist failed to mention that the cadaver he had examined was that of the sergeant shot down in the street. There was an absence of a link between the evidence the pathologist gave and the man the accused was charged with murdering. There was no continuity in the evidence and because of this failing the case was dismissed. The spin-off from this legal argument is that now there has to be a 'continuity officer'; that is someone who saw the victim, say of a road accident, had their body identified, had them certified dead and then identified to the pathologist before the postmortem. In this way the pathologist can then say that he carried out the autopsy on Mr or Mrs So and So who had been involved in an accident at such and such a place and at such a time and day.

Because of the number of fatal accidents I had to deal with during my service there were many times when I had to identify the body to the pathologist. Once this was done I was free to leave the mortuary but on many occasions I was invited to watch the examination. Francis Camps, later Sir Francis, was keen to show me what he was doing and why and more importantly what he was looking for. In was not morbid interest on my part; I was keen to see the top pathologist at work and Francis Camps answered the many questions I put to him. It would be an in-depth discussion and we developed a good rapport.

He was the man who did the examination on the valet that had hung himself on that lovely warm summer Sunday and explained to me what had happened and his reasoning behind his findings.

It was years later when I had taken my eldest son, who was about nine at the time to see the film 'The Battle of Britain' at the Odeon, Tottenham Court Road.

On route to Gravesend at Tottenham Court Road underground station Sir Francis Camps was there on the platform with his daughter about the same age as my son and invited us back to his home for a drink. I had to decline this offer explaining that I had to get to Charing Cross then a train to Gravesend and a bus to Higham to get my son back to his mother.

One of the stories he related to me, during our many hours together, was that of an examination he had to carry out on the body of a fifteen year old girl. This was in Jersey and the young girl had been strangled. His examination showed that her anal sphincter had been damaged over a period of time showing that she had been buggered on many occasions. From this he concluded that the mother of the girl would have been aware of the laxity of the girl's bottom as it would have been obvious from the state of her panties. He then concluded that the mother was aware of what was going on and had chosen to ignore it for whatever reason and it therefore pointed to a member of the family being the culprit. Sir Francis passed his findings onto the investigating officers and in fact the girl's cousin was arrested, charged and found guilty. It is safe to assume that the young lady was fed up being buggered and refused any further actions of this sort. The cousin most likely insisted and was physically refused and most likely threatened with exposure, so he strangled the poor girl.

One pathologist I met at Farnborough Hospital Mortuary asked me to stay after I had identified the body of a young lady, who had died as the result of being a passenger in a car that had collided, in the early hours of the morning, with a Green Line bus. I had examined her at the scene, an discovered that her abdomen was 'board like' indicating internal haemorrhage. I was on my way to work when I came across this accident. At the hospital the casualty officer treated her for a fractured skull. The casualty officer arrived at the mortuary where the pathologist showed him the ruptured liver caused by the impact and the skull which had no injury. The young doctor left having the error of his ways pointed out to him. The pathologist said that if he had properly diagnosed the girl's injury, opened her up and stitched her liver up she would still be alive.

Ron Cross and I one afternoon, at the beginning of the evening rush hour, were called to an accident that had taken place at the south side of Wandsworth Bridge, where a woman riding a moped had gone under the rear wheels of a large lorry carrying thirty tons of aggregate. The rear wheels had come to rest across her lower pelvis and upper thighs which were compressed by the weight to about one inch. The woman was fully conscious and asked had a doctor been called, to which, solely to reassure her, I said yes. I knew that the weight of the vehicle had crushed all the bones in that region and the blood vessels would be ruptured so that she could feel no pain because of the lack of blood to her nerves in that part of her body. I also knew that once the weight had been removed, the shock to her system, coupled with the fact that the blood supply to her body would disappear out of her injured pelvis, would be fatal,

I discovered from her where she lived which was only a few streets away and set off to tell her father, with whom she lived, what had happened. The house which was in a line of terraced houses opened directly onto the pavement. I should add at this point that the fire brigade had arrived, jacked the lorry up and the woman had died.

I knocked on the door and it was opened by her father who was blind. The conversation that now follows happened as quickly as you read it.

'Mr So and So?'

'Yes. Are you a policeman?'

'Yes.'

'Has she had an accident?'

'Yes.'

'Is she dead?'

'Yes.'

'I knew it would happen and soon as she bought that motorcycle. Come in and I'll make you a cup of tea.'

To watch him making a cup of tea, knowing the news I had just given him had not yet really sunk in, was very moving. I asked him whether he wanted me to inform Social Services but he declined saying that his neighbours would look after him.

Part Five

Accidents and incidents.
Metropolitan Police Motor Cycle Precision Team.
The Special Escort Group and the various escorts undertaken.
Characters met, remembered and some best forgotten.

THE PRECISION TEAM

I had been at the garage for about fifteen months when I was approached in the canteen by Chalkie White and Tom Lucas, and asked if I would like to join the Precision Team. They stated that a high standard of tidiness and motorcycle riding was required, and they thought that I might join them. I thought it over and decided to do so. I became a reserve in the team which meant that I had to learn all the positions ridden by the others members so that if they were sick, on holiday, or elsewhere I could take over their place.

There were eight riding members made up into two groups of four, which in effect had to perform a mirror image, one with the other. Chalkie White led one half of the team with Tom leading the other four.

The display was not one of trick riding, although I'm certain that we could have out-performed most trick riding motorcycle teams. Ours was of a precision display, showing the control of powerful motorcycles at slow and fast speeds.

The display which had been structured mainly by Tom lasted about fifteen minutes in good conditions, but on wet grass could last as long as twenty.

We trained at Warren Police Club sports ground at Hayes in Kent, but after a short while we managed to have facilities at the end of the main runway on Biggin Hill Airfield. We would train every day during the summer until we had things to perfection, moving as one and turning as one.

Sergeant Lofty Lay was the team manager, who was there to organize our duties, enabling us to work as a team. We were invited to the Triumph Motorcycle Factory Sports Day at Meriden. We travelled there in the back of a large lorry, with the bikes in another.

The display was a complete and utter shambles. The ground we rode on had recently had turf laid down on it, so when the team hit the brakes, the ground moved like loose carpet tiles. Making us become disorientated which ended up looking more like a farce. We decided that in the future all rides must be practised on the actual grounds first, before the show. In the case of wet grass or a greasy surface, Chalkie White as the leader would have to adjust the pace of the ride to suit the conditions.

While crossing the square you also had to avoid the other team coming at you from the other corner. The secret of our success was we all had only one rider to look out for. If he wasn't there you didn't go down the line. If you hadn't moved into position for whatever reason, like a wheel spin or something like that, the chap who was to cross over behind you just didn't go.

We did have one incident when Ron Cross and Ron Dargan collided at a display in North London, which made headlines in the Daily Mirror the following day.

Fortunately nobody was injured and with only a short delay we were back on our way.

The first display we did was led by our new sergeant, at St. Mary's Hospital, Sidcup. We went into the arena after the fire brigade had done their display. Johnny Baldwin's four had to form a reasonably tight circle. Johnny fell off when the bike slipped away from underneath him. Such was his debut, but he persevered and we got over the problem and it was back to business as usual.

Under the supervision of Superintendent Tom Couchman, well over six foot tall and as bald as a coot, the Precision Team went to Hanover, in Germany to represent the British in an International Police Exhibition. We stayed at a small hotel to the north of Hanover and did most our displays at the Fleurplatz on the outskirts. I led the team while Jock Shields stood back and relaxed. It was a grass surface and the rides went well. Also at this place was a static display of Messerschmitt helicopters that had the unusual feature of the main rotor blades being driven by compressed air at the extreme tips. There were also one or two other items on display which had a link to the police work that had to be performed.

Asked to do a small sample of our display on a walkway at the side of the lake, I concocted a single narrow move where the two lots of four came towards the camera (this was for German television). Starting off side-by-side they would then interweave one with another as they approached the critical point. What it finally looked like I have no idea but it appeared to satisfy the lady producer, who was a real beauty.

We had to go to the Main Arena in Hanover that apparently had been instigated by the infamous Herman Goering and was a beautiful showground with a lake there. We were not entitled to ride on the public roads in Hanover but this problem was got round by the German police escorting us as a very tight bunch from the Fleurplatz to the main arena. There we had to perform in front of a large crowd.

There were contingents from most of the European countries and all showed off their various abilities. One that sticks in my mind was the Italian Police Band; fantastic musicians and led by a man on horseback. I would now like to describe him in some detail as I had a close view of him when the German television were filming. I will start with the horse: to say that it had seen better days would be an understatement. Although it looked well and was well groomed it lacked something: a sense of well-being could be the point. The saddle and gear on the horse had never seen saddle soap or polish in its lifetime and the bear skin, there must be a name for it but I've no idea what it is, was suffering from a chronic touch of the mange. Sitting astride this beast was the man of all seasons, he had overindulged himself, was large in stature and had a blue unshaven chin and sat on the horse like a sack of shit tied in the middle. His eyes never left the young lady from the television crew and he could easily have been convicted of rape just by the look on his face. To conclude on this particular man, he had a touch of the theatricals about him and would not have looked out of place in a comic opera.

Come the grand show in this arena Jock Shields pulled rank and insisted that he should lead the team, much against the wishes of the team members who would have preferred that I did the job. We had one other complication before we could do our obligatory practise ride. In the main arena they had set up three posts for the tug of war final and they refused to move them as Tom Couchman had requested. However I had a few words with those in charge and after retuning to Tom saw police cadets removing the posts. I was asked what I had said to them and stated that unless the posts were removed we would go home. I stuck my neck out on this point but it achieved the desired result.

The final night at our hotel was most enjoyable and schnapps was consumed in large quantities. The following morning we set off for home with me having a somewhat disturbed stomach (due to the schnapps). At Harwich a Special Branch officer came onto the ferry and shepherded us through the customs, in fact we by-passed them all together with the Special Branch man signalling to the customs officer that we would be going straight to the train en route for Liverpool Street. This had been arranged on our way out to Germany where liaising with the customs and knowing that we would not be taking advantage of the facility, the Special Branch man did as he said: come on board to look after us. It was a much appreciated gesture and made the journey that much easier.

In 1971 the Metropolitan Police were invited to give a display at the Agricultural Showground at Stoneleigh. It was to last an hour, from four p.m. to five p.m. and was to take place in the main arena.

Assistant Commissioner Jim Starritt was in charge. Those taking part were to be the Metropolitan Police Band, the cadets from the Cadet Training School, Mounted Branch doing a musical ride, dog handlers and the Precision Team. We had to attend a briefing by the Assistant Commissioner at Scotland Yard. We were in the briefing room when a chief superintendent came onto the stage to say that Mr Starritt would be coming to address us shortly. Jim Starritt entered and then in his Ulster accent told us that he wanted forty dogs and their handlers, forty motorcyclists and forty horses. I piped up that the maximum we could train and more importantly contain in the arena was sixteen, to which he said, 'Alright, sixteen it is'. He then gave us a bullshit lecture and left the stage. The chief superintendent then came on to say that he was disappointed that no one stood up when the Assistant Commissioner came on. There was a pause and then from the back of the amphitheatre came, 'Bollocks'. Big cheers from everyone and the stage was rapidly evacuated by the man who considered that he could address us almost as school children.

As the team consisted of ten members already, that is eight members and two reserves, we enrolled volunteers from the Special Escort Group to make up the sixteen riding members and again two reserves. As Sergeant Jock Shields already led the team another sergeant joined us to lead the back half of the team and we also had an Inspector West join us to make up the full complement of those in charge and those doing the display.

I set out to alter the display we had been doing for years and spent many hours drawing up a new sequence which had to last for twenty minutes. I did drawings of the various moves and added notes to the drawings to put into words how the move should and would have to be, performed. Having completed the drawings I then went into the CID office at Lewisham and used up all their copying paper doing eighteen copies. These were then stapled together and each member of the team received one. (I still have the original with the glaring spelling mistake on the front cover. In freehand and in pencil I had written Metropitan Police Motor Cycle Precision team; you can see that Metropolitan is misspelt. Underneath was our unauthorised badge of a winged motorcycle with the crown above it. We did one year have Christmas cards printed with this design on it. I had done the original drawing for Chalkie White whose father had a printing business in Walthamstow.

We started our rehearsals at Biggin Hill with every move being walked first and then slowly ridden until we managed to get it right. One of the new moves had to be slightly amended because the movements for it went out of sequence as it went on. This was where we had two opposing motorcyclists passing each other as they went through a turning circle of the other eight. As the circle turned the next two would go through, but what was happening was that as the eight to go through the circle had gone to their points those towards the tail-end would have had to become stationary before their time to cross came along. This would never do, so I had them keep moving up the sides of the arena until the point where they had to cross came along. The man marking the crossing point was Jock Shields wearing a red sash; in fact both sergeants wore these as it helped identify them more easily.

While training them I would insist that as they moved along behind each other, from the front I would only want to see one motorcyclist. They were very good and became a very capable and competent sixteen.

A dress rehearsal was to take place at Imber Court with Jim Starritt there and Her Majesty the Queen arriving with a very young Prince Andrew by helicopter. On her arrival she spent time with the Mounted Branch and some time with the dogs but ignored the motorcycles altogether. It may be that we were a noisy bunch.

Jim Starritt came up to me, and bear in mind that I knew him as a junior inspector at Marylebone Lane, and in his well mannered way asked, 'What fiddle are you on?' I said that I trained the motorcycle display team. He said nothing and just walked away.

The display was to be during the period of the 6th to the 9th of July 1971 and at Stoneleigh we were lodged in the campus of a college nearby which was very close to a council estate. We had individual rooms and the food was first class.

Inspector West stated that as he came from that neck of the woods he had organised a party for us at some club or other. The beer would be cheap, as would the food and that there would be lots of female company. Most of the contingent went off to this paradise to find that it was a Working Men's Club, the beer was a penny a pint dearer, the food consisted of stale cheese rolls and the female company consisted of mature ladies, most being Old Age Pensioners. We didn't stay long and a young Mounted Branch man and I decided we would organise a 'do' on the campus. We involved the dance band section of the band and the Mounted Branch put on a skit of our display, borrowing children's scooters and tricycles from the nearby council tenants, hence them being mentioned earlier. We sang one or two ditties taking the piss out of the Mounted Branch and the band played a very wide selection of music. With them they had a ginger-haired sergeant from Greenwich, who had a glorious tenor voice. He had in fact been trained at La Scala, Milan but suffered the most agonising stage fright so he became a policeman. He sang two Arias and appeared to enjoy showing off his ability or gift and was well applauded at the end.

Mounted Branch commented that they could not stay long as they had to be up early to 'muck out' and prepare their tack and the horses for the day ahead. They referred to us as lucky bastards as we could lay in bed till midday if we so wished and didn't have to be at the showground until after lunch. They suggested that the display team come down to the stables in the morning and try out their horses and we agreed that the following day after breakfast we would come down to the ground. We did this and on disembarking from the coach were met by two constables on horseback wearing nothing more than swimming trunks and carrying lances who then marched us off to the stables where all the horses were prepared and ready for us. We rode their horses and they rode our bikes and a good time was had by all.

The chief inspector of Mounted Branch knowing that I was the trainer of the motorcyclists said that my job was easy as I only had to train sixteen men while he had to train sixteen men and sixteen horses for their musical ride.

Come the day of the first display and we found that at our appointed time to enter the arena the 'Hunter Class' was still being judged, in fact the judges were congregating to discuss various points but they were encroaching on our allotted time; we had to enter the arena at four and leave at five. The Mounted Branch chief inspector was under the grandstand waiting for us to commence the display. We had an hour and no longer and we had to get in the arena on time and leave it an hour later. It was causing some concern to the chief inspector and I chose to go over to the head judge of the Hunter Class to ask him to vacate the arena. This I did and he was most apologetic. I had arranged that as soon as the horses left the arena, a tractor complete with heavy roller would go over the arena to flatten it and get rid of the divots the horses hooves had kicked. Having arranged that I returned to the chief inspector under the grandstand who asked what the judge had said. I said he apologised and I thanked him for so doing. Once the ground was flattened the display commenced and went off without a hitch. The Precision Team performed well and I stood at the front of the arena while they performed. I was ready to bring on the reserves if someone's bike broke down or if someone collided or fell off. We were ready for any eventuality and the reserves had been trained to ride in any position.

After us came the dog handlers who marched in a eight abreast, forming five ranks. They then called on their dogs to sit which they did as the handlers marched to the far side of the arena. One dog, I think he was named Grey Ghost, an obscure German breed when told to sit would sit and when the handler had moved on, would defecate to the cheers of all the policemen watching. This happened every time they entered the arena. The dog was obviously suffering from stage fright, had a looseness of the bowels or, being German in origin, misunderstood the command 'sit'.

The whole display was a great success with the cadets doing their physical training display and the Mounted Branch, who finished off the show, doing their musical ride.

We had two, what can only be described as camp followers, absolutely gorgeous to look at and employed so I reasoned out, as staff at Scotland Yard. They were not for the likes of us ordinary constables, or even for the rank conscious sergeants but accompanied those of higher rank.

What is very sad, and this is where the powers that be fall down, there was never a note of appreciation for all the hard work that had gone into what was for many reasons very complimentary to the Metropolitan Police.

Every few years or so, the Triumph Motor Cycle company produced a new model and in one particular year produced a machine for the Metropolitan Police with the title of Saint. It was the normal standard motorcycle with variations suitable for our work. The engine was fitted with a Bonneville head and cylinder barrels and it had a single carburettor and the lower gear had been reduced to give us the ability to move at walking pace without having to use the clutch. The team went to the police garage at Merton to collect the machines. We were allocated our individual machines and ran them gently back to Lewisham where we then set about running them in and improving their appearance by polishing them down to a lustrous finish. To run them in we would, individually, set out on long runs with them. This was not always within the Metropolitan Police district but out into the counties. We would ring up the local headquarters of a constabulary and ask their permission to pass through their ground. This was always given and we would set out on a long purposeful ride involving many miles. I always took the opportunity to visit relatives when after, say, two hours' gentle riding one could stop for an hour, let the bike cool down and enjoy the company, of say, my brother and his family at Westgate in Kent or my great uncle and aunt (here I had been an evacuee during the early years of the war) near Aylesbury in Buckinghamshire. In this way the machines bedded down to a nice silky purr and the exhaust pipes didn't become blued.

Back at the garage we would set about rubbing down the sand-cast crankcase with emery paper and paraffin, gradually rendering it down to a highly polished finish with the use of Solvo Autosol, and finally jewellers' rouge: a powder that didn't leave a bloom on the aluminium castings. Wheels would be taken out and polished and the Amal carburettor came in for such treatment that it shone like a jewel.

There was also the chance that we might fall off them so the underside was also polished. The technique we used for the nuts holding the cylinder to the crankcase was to remove, one at a time, the nuts and washers, holding them there, polish the copper washer and then the nut and replace them to the correct torque. At the end of all this treatment they shone and we knew exactly whether everything was in order; no loose nuts or whatever.

I was asked by Superintendent Bill Fleming if I was willing to be interviewed by Drive Magazine, the periodical of the Institute of Advanced motorists. I agreed and was interviewed at Scotland Yard where I was chaperoned by another superintendent. After about an hour it was all over and my chaperone only butted in once when he said, 'You can't say that,' when I had referred to the treatment afforded to motorcyclists by the ordinary motorist. I pointed out that if I was being interviewed as a motorist I would have held a contrary view. It went well and in the ensuing publication it stated Jim Goodwin, longest serving member of the Special Escort Group and trainer of the internationally famous Precision Team said, 'Concentration is essential.' That was all but what was gratifying was that Lord Brabazon agreed; a keen motorcyclist and coincidently the first man ever in the British Isles to have a private pilot's licence.

THE PRECISION TEAM ADVENTURES IN AMSTERDAM

The Precision Team was invited to take part in a military tattoo to be held in Amsterdam as part of the British Week being held to foster the good relations that exist between the British and the Dutch. It was also being held to foster trade between the two countries.

We were to take part in a military display at the RAI Exhibition Centre in Amsterdam, and we were to be billeted in a barracks five miles from the centre.

Johnny Baldwin, the sergeant who had been leading the team was unable to go as he had to attend an interview board for the next rank up. In consequence yours truly as first reserve and trainer had to ride in the lead position.

Everyone apart from Ron Cross, myself, the mechanic Tug Wilson were travelling from Liverpool Street Station to Harwich and then on by boat to the Hook of Holland and then onto Amsterdam by train.

I had volunteered to travel with the bikes and to organize their passage through customs and their safe arrival into Holland.

When we got to the barracks we found that there had been a bit of a contretemps with the sergeant major who was in charge of the billeting arrangements. We had been informed by Bill Fleming, our superintendent, that we were to be treated as the equivalent rank of warrant officers or sergeants, and so allotted facilities comparable to those ranks. However, the lads on their arrival were shown a barrack room containing members of the Parachute Regiment. To say that it was substandard would be putting it mildly. The ablution was flooded and it was a complete arse of a place.

In consequence the lads informed the sergeant major that no way were they having those quarters, and he was so informed by Stan Gammon to 'fuck off.' He then went off to find the adjutant and was told in no uncertain manner that he could do what he liked.

The team found the officers' quarters and we took up residence there in three rooms. Each room contained two pairs of bunk beds.

Bill Fleming quite rightly accepted that the original accommodation was unsuitable, and he was apprehensive about how we would conduct ourselves in the presence of the military officers.

He hadn't needed to worry as the officers reported that the conduct had been first class and they had enjoyed their time spent there.

Time passed by and we found ourselves readying for the event in which we had come to perform. We marked out the arena in the RAI hall and got on with our rehearsals. At this point I should mention that the military attaché at the British Embassy at The Hague had thought that the display we were going to do was on road safety. After watching our rehearsal, we were moved up into the prime spot, just before the finale.

The first rehearsal went well apart from the fact that I repeated one move about four times, with the whole team following me behind; they had known what had happened and stayed calm until I got my mind cleared and then we commenced. The fact that we were riding inside and on a concrete arena enabled us to speed up certain moves, while allowing slower moves to be done more sedately, so giving a better show of our control of the machines at both slow and fast speeds. We did five rides in total, all of which I'm pleased to say went well and we were well received by our audience. Apparently the men were standing up applauding while in some of the faster moves the ladies were hiding their eyes. All-in-all a great success with the machines never letting us down, and the team members thoroughly enjoying themselves. We were later complimented for a job well done by the British Ambassador in Holland, who remarked that we were sensational.

Amsterdam is famed for many things. Windmills are very common and are still being used in the countryside by the farmers. Tulips are also something that comes to mind, growing freely and also on sale at the beautiful flower markets. Cheese is very popular, and comes in all shapes, sizes and smells, and as you walk by the cheese shops you may find yourself holding your nose.

There is of course the Van Gogh Museum, with many of his fine works on display. Van Gogh only ever sold one painting for $100 in his lifetime. None of his work became famous until he died in 1890 at the age of forty-three. You can even visit Ann Frank's home, the young girl that hid from the Germans during the war behind a makeshift bookcase in the attic.

Bicycles come in the thousand, as the streets are narrow and many are cobble-stoned, and surround all the canals and bridges.

You can't of course go to Amsterdam without experiencing its famed 'Red Light District,' where you can easily pick a beautiful girl to spend a lustful half an hour with, and to do whatever you so desire.

If you were to come from the train station as I did, you would find that the district is quite close by. You can quite easily find yourself lost if you're not careful as the streets in this neighbourhood are very narrow, and lead into other back streets that twist and turn all over the place. You don't have to worry about it being too dark as it's lit, well dimly lit, by all the red florescent lighting coming from the prostitutes' doors and windows.

One night we took the opportunity to explore the streets but of course we all denied any knowledge of it.

For instance, Ron Cross came back to the cafe and we asked him where he had been, and he told us that he hadn't been anywhere, but he had eyes that looked like piss holes in the snow, not to mention that he also looked exhausted.

Stan Gammon came back a bit cross after he told us that he thought he was having two women and only had one. So much for the old hush-hush from him.

Another one of the lads told us that after he dipped his whistle, he nabbed back his money that he had paid the girl when she wasn't looking. I guess he wasn't very happy with the service and thought that he should get a refund, or so he said he did.

We were all prone to sprucing up our stories in those days, as a certain defence mechanism, as you must never show any signs of weakness.

I was still recovering from my disastrous rehearsal from that day, and so having an air of nervous tension about me was unable to function, not forgetting to mention that there was a little mutt in the room and I'm not talking about the two-legged kind. She pulled out one of her vibrating sex toys which practically put me to sleep; most relaxing.

Now remember I deny everything about that night as well as did all my fellow officers.

On the ferry back, we ran into the Highland Regiment and of course they were all wearing kilts, and in the traditional way, with nothing underneath, which was a bit of an embarrassment. With their legs spread out wide, their tackle was on display for all eyes too see. One of their superior officers came back to tell them to be a bit more demure in their blessed scene.

AIR SHOWS

As a means of saying thank you to the people at Biggin Hill we did displays at the Battle of Britain Day and at the air fair. It was while we were training for the Battle of Britain display that we met up with the Black Arrows RAF display team who had flown in to take part in the display. We practisced in front of their tent on the apron where we would be performing the following day. Comments were passed and they held the view that what we did was more dangerous than what they did. They based this on the fact that we were restricted in taking avoiding action by the fact that we could only swerve or brake, they could go down or up or sideways. We managed to get some of them to sit on the back of the bikes during a trial run and they thoroughly enjoyed it. We also had the Daimler Dart there and we gave a joy ride to one or two of them flat out up the main runway.

They flew the Hawker Hunter and years later when the Folland Gnat was the plane, Johnny Baldwin was invited to go up with them during their show but he declined. When I heard of this I said that I'd have loved to have gone up but by this time the necessary arrangements and kitting out couldn't be done.

At one of the air fairs some of the lads were given a ride in a Royal Marine helicopter which apparently hovered over a couple who were at it like rattlesnakes on a grassy bank just away from the airfield. The girl spotted them first, which was quite natural really as she was the only one facing the sky. It took her a few minutes to interrupt her partner who must have died the death on looking up to see the helicopter above.

The Decca Air Navigation Systems had a De Haviland Prince aircraft at Biggin Hill which was equipped with all their latest equipment and was used to give demonstration flights to prospective customers. We were at the end of the runway when this plane taxied down and turned ready to take off. The pilot stuck his head out of the cockpit window and gave us a two fingered salute. We returned it in kind but when we saw that he was persisting I discovered that he was signalling that he had room for two passengers, so during the training sessions we would in turn go off for a forty minute flight over the Isle of Wight or wherever. I clocked, I think that's the right expression, about sixteen hours flying in this way and had the opportunity to sit in the co-pilot's seat when Decca had some highly perfumed Japanese on board.

Bill Fleming turned up one day at the same time that the plane turned and prepared to take on two non-paying passengers. Again the pilot was persistent and in the end we cajoled Bill Fleming to go up. As soon as he was airborne we disappeared back to the garage. We found out later that from the moment he left the ground to the time he landed the poor chap was sick all the time.

It was fascinating to see the plane operate under the automatic system, John, the pilot would push a button above the windscreen and the plane would then fly a circuit out to the Isle of Wight and bring us back to the end of the runway at Biggin Hill. Such things were in their infancy and how it worked was and still, is, beyond my understanding.

We used to enter Biggin Hill Airfield by the main RAF gate and make our way to the training area via the various taxiways. This was always done at high speed and we would race each other through the various bends. As this was indeed noisy at the best of times the RAF requested us to use the private entrance as we would disturb the potential officer recruits for the RAF.

ESCORT DUTIES

Of all the escort duties I was involved in, the group that comes most happily to mind are the leaders of Ghana. The first I came into contact with was when he was in London attending the Commonwealth Prime Ministers' Conference. His name was Nkrumah and he had a great leaning towards the Soviets. During his stay he resided at the Ghanaian High Commissioner's official residence in St John's Wood.

The two Special Branch officers who had charge of his security were Mike Davies and Jock Wilson and they had a further six or so Special Branch officers with them. Apart from having to change the route to Lancaster House there were no problems and Stan Gammon and I managed to get him wherever he had to be, on time and with a smooth uninterrupted run.

He returned to Ghana after the conference and while making an official visit to Guinea was ousted and John Harlley took over the leadership of the country. It was he who arrived at the next Commonwealth conference and during his visit stayed at the Carlton Towers Hotel off Sloane Street. Mike Davies was again in charge of the security aspect of the visit and the Ghanaian leader invited us all, Special Branch and the two motorcyclists, to use the facilities at the hotel as his guests. He was a most pleasant man to meet and we did appreciate his hospitality. This visit was during the Rhodesian troubles and on one occasion Mike Davies asked if I could arrange to have a car to take John Harlley and his wife out into the countryside to get away from demonstrations that were threatened because of Rhodesia. I arranged through Superintendent Fitzpatrick to have the use of the nondescript Triumph 2000 car. I was in plain clothes with Mike Davies sitting next to me and our distinguished passengers in the back seat. John Harlley had expressed a wish to see rivers and reservoirs as he pointed out his village in Ghana always suffered from drought. I took them up through Buckinghamshire and visited many places where water was in abundance and after lunch at a local hotel near Aylesbury we ambled back to the Carlton Towers Hotel with no demonstrators to be seen. Apparently other teams with their prime ministers were under siege all day.

We had a very good arrangement for the midday meal at the hotel. Before we set off for Lancaster House we would select the dishes we wanted for luncheon; a starter, main course and perhaps a dessert. This would be left with the Special Branch man who was protecting the hotel rooms of the guests. When we were about to leave to come back for this prearranged meal, the Special Branch man in the foyer of the hotel would be telephoned via Scotland Yard that we were about to leave, he would then inform the man on the protection duty on our floor and he would then ring room service on the internal phone and place our order. By the time we arrived at the hotel, made our way up via the service lift we had only a few minutes before two trolleys arrived with our chosen delicacies. Each of us gave the waiters half a crown; it was very good value and the waiters were also delighted with the arrangement.

While we were enjoying ourselves as the guest of the Prime Minister from Ghana others, for whatever reason, had declined the hospitality of their ward and were having the traditional fry-up at Cannon Row Police Station canteen.

The three years passed between the conferences for the Commonwealth prime ministers and the next Ghanaian arrived. It was General Ankrah, Chairman of the Liberation Front for Ghana who had been elected to the post. A man of short stature but of the new school of prime ministers for his country. Again Mike Davies was the man in charge of the Special Branch team and had now risen to the rank of detective chief inspector. Like John Harlley, General Ankrah stayed at the Carlton Towers Hotel and again we were invited to accept their hospitality, which we did. My first face-to-face contact with him was when Mike Davies came into the room to say that the General wished to see me. We had by this time arranged, through room service, for a bottle of Black Label to be delivered to our room. The General duly arrived and asked me if I was a pilot. I asked him in turn why did he ask that, to which he replied, 'You were flying down the motorway.' I replied that it was my wish that we should get him to the hotel as quickly as possible so that he could relax before the conference that was to start the following day. He enquired as to what I liked to drink and I said Black Label whiskey. He then ordered a bottle via room service, we having denied all knowledge of how this could be done and that was that.

The following morning his Ghanaian body guards came into the room with duty-free cigarettes and a bottle of Dutch whiskey with the title of Always Mellow. We, of course offered them a drink and they opted for the Black Label that was on display. This we gave them and then decided that we would empty the Black Label bottle and decant the Always Mellow into the empty Black Label bottle. Every morning during the stay the bodyguards came in with more cigarettes and more Always Mellow, again we would offer them a drink, as was the custom and they would opt for the Black Label, which in fact was Always Mellow. If we wished to drink with them we would go to the bathroom and appear with a glass of Black Label that was secreted there.

General Ankrah had received his training at Sandhurst and prior to his visit had intimated that he wished to visit the Academy. I set out with 202TD Timber Woods, known with great affection as the Talking Ring Spanner, to go over the route. We were both in plain clothes and were driving the Triumph 2000 that I previously mentioned. Timber had a clipboard and my Ingersol pocket watch to time us over various stages. The idea was that we would mentally note places where there could be hold-ups, congestion or whatever and then places on the route where we could get a move on, to make up lost time and other places where we could slow so as not to inconvenience other road users. On the route in question there is a level crossing and we timed its closing and opening to discover what period of time had elapsed. We needed to know these things before escorting the General to Sandhurst. At Bagshot Timber we turned into the Military Academy grounds and stopped at the main, grand colonnaded, entrance where we were met by a porter who enquired as to who we were and I introduced us as Mister Goodwin and Mister Woods of the Metropolitan Police Special Escort Group. This introduction warranted the adjutant being called. Duly arriving he looked the part, his uniform was bleached khaki, riding breeches with riding boots and a sam brown, with all leather highly polished, and to go with it a clipped military voice, which is what one would have expected from the adjutant of the Royal Military Academy at Sandhurst. He welcomed us and then set about us in style.

'I don't want any of the nonsense we had with the German chappie. He arrived ten minutes too early and the CO had to be fetched.

I stated that we were due to arrive at twelve noon and at twelve noon we would arrive. At that point he invited us to coffee in the officers' mess and we accepted his invitation and spent about half an hour imbibing coffee beautifully presented and humbly served by the mess stewards. I had prewarned Timber that we restrict ourselves to the simplest of conversation as I knew full well why Timber had the nickname of the Talking Ring Spanner.

Come the actual escort and I had Harry Waterson from Barnes garage with me. We enjoyed the job and on going to Sandhurst we turned off at Bagshot to enter the grounds of the Military Academy with six minutes to spare. We had a slow ceremonial drive up to the grand entrance just as the clock over the portico came up to twelve noon. Things changed slightly from my reconnoitring visit: no longer in the officers' mess having coffee but in a basement room next to the boiler house. Mike Davies was with us when a porter arrived and addressing Mike said, 'Inspector Davies?'

Mike replied, 'Detective Inspector Davies.'

The porter then said, 'Detective Inspector Davies?'

Mike said, 'Detective Chief Inspector Davies. Yes, what can I do for you?'

'The adjutant would like you to have lunch with him.'

To which Mike said, 'That's very kind of him and I would be pleased to join him once I have seen my two men here fed and watered.'

This was soon done with army corned beef sandwiches and a mug of tea.

While on this particular escort I had a visit from Jock Shields, in a sort of supervisory capacity whom, after a few glasses of Black Label, I ushered down the service lift to the baggage hall where I arranged for an open sandwich to be produced. He ate the lot and disappeared off to Bow garage, from whence he came, at such a speed that he could be still be heard when I arrived back on the tenth floor. We could then settle down to normality again and relax.

Nowadays the Commonwealth Prime Ministers' Conferences are held every three years at different Commonwealth capitals and they longer have to be catered for in London.

One of the basic requirements of someone doing Escort Duty is that one should always be discreet and be aware that there are those out there who would just love to get their teeth into something that may make headlines in the newspapers. There is also the question of people being envious of one's good fortune. An example of this is where a member of the Escort Group relates to his wife what a fantastic time he has had; for example the meals he had while a guest of a head of state. The wife then talks to another policeman's wife who wants to know why her husband doesn't enjoy the same. Letters are written and phone calls made and trouble starts. You had to keep to yourself what you did, what had happened and how you were treated. This was the secret of success and with it went the fact that you could be relied on.

There were two occasions when I had the task of escorting a funeral procession and they were tasks that required a more concentrated form of decorum than the normal escort. I'm not saying that decorum was absent at other times, but with a funeral there was more of a beginning, and certainly when nearing our destination, more of an end.

The first was the funeral of Clement Attlee who in the War Cabinet had been deputy Prime Minister under Churchill. At the end of the war he was leader of the Labour Party and became Prime Minister of the Labour Government. He was of the old school of politicians, very caring for the general good of everyone and devoted to the job in hand.

When he died the funeral service was held at the small church in Lincoln Inn and from there he had to be taken to Roehampton Crematorium. We left the Church and moved at an appropriate pace down onto the embankment along to Lambeth Bridge and once over that we speeded up slightly in order to get to Roehampton on time. Once we arrived within a mile of the destination we then slowed to a respectful funeral pace and once there, Ron Cross and I parked behind the building out of sight to have a quiet respectful fag on the strength of having arrived on time and with nothing untoward happening on route.

So as not to disturb the service going on inside we waited till everyone had left before starting our bikes and making our way back to Lewisham.

The other funeral I had to deal with, insofar as I had to escort the funeral party from Westminster Abbey again to Roehampton, was the funeral of Sir Joseph Simpson who died in office while serving as the Commissioner of Police. I was asked by Superintendent Bill Fleming to arrange the escort and I was to be accompanied by another motorcyclist, and for the life of me I cannot remember his name. Before the actual day the pair of us went to the funeral directors in Ladbrooke Grove to discuss how we would proceed once we left the Abbey. I suggested that once the coffin had been brought out and placed in the hearse we would form up some hundred yards ahead in order to make a sharp right turn to go down the wrong side of Parliament Square. We would then move down to the House of Commons, turn right again, with foot duty holding up the traffic, slow pace to Lambeth Bridge, over it at the same pace and then speed up when we were on the south side of the river. As before, with Clement Attlee, all went well on the day. I had arranged that we would be parked in the Abbey Gardens out of sight but would be signalled by two PCs when movement was afoot, one outside the Abbey door and the other one by the entrance to the gardens, who would give us the nod. In this way we discreetly started our machines and slowly moved out into our start positions. Again everything went according to plan.

I was late turn on motorcycle duty at Lewisham when the duty sergeant informed me that he had an escort for me to carry out. Namely to escort Princess Alexander and Angus Ogilvy, together with their guest, the Persian Princess, from Queen's Theatre in the Haymarket to Thatched House Lodge in Richmond Park. It was suggested that I took some assistance with me and I asked a comparatively young and new recruit to Traffic to join me, as I thought it would be a wonderful experience for him.

When we arrived in the Haymarket there were about five Rolls Royces to escort. I then explained to my young colleague what we would do: namely leap-frog, passing each other the junctions along the route which I had outlined to him. We set out and arrived safely at Richmond Park where the night duty officer there opened the gates to the driveway to Thatched House Lodge. I should mention, that while overtaking the cavalcade to get to the next junction I noticed in one of the limousines a young lady complete with tiara and fur coat, illuminated in the back of the car who smiled at me every time I overtook her vehicle, with this great throbbing motorcycle between my thighs.

On arrival Angus Ogilvy came over to the pair of us and explained that he had laid on supper for us in the butler's pantry. I thanked him for his kindness and mentioned that we had met once before, when I escorted the new husband and wife back from Gatwick after their honeymoon in South Africa. Cheekily I also asked him who the delightful young lady was in such and such a car. He said that it was Princess So and So from Wherever, and left us to our supper. It was a selection of cold meats, stilton cheese, pickles and every sort of wind-inducing nourishment. It was accompanied by beer or if you so wanted, a fine collection of single malt whiskeys were there. Just after one o'clock in the morning the butler entered, and said that she was going back to the Embassy. So out we go and start to put on our motorcycle gear. It was a moonlit summer's night, when Mr Ogilvy came over to us and asked if supper was to our liking. I said, 'First class, sir.' To which he said that if it hadn't been he would have sacked the butler, and as a passing aside said, 'By the way you made a bit of a hit with Princess So and So of Wherever.'

Anyway the end to this story is that we escorted the Persian Princess back to Princes Gate and made our way home. In these circumstances the night duty car would be out patrolling and the garage locked up, so we took the bikes home and took them to the garage later the following day. It would be then that I would inform the sergeant of the time we finished the escort and arrived home.

One of the escort jobs Ron Cross and I had to undertake was the escort of a prison van containing the Krays from Brixton prison, where they were on remand, to Bow Street Magistrates' Court for their committal proceedings. The man in charge of the investigation was Nipper Read. I'd known him at Paddington Green Police Station when I was aid to CID. We chatted away about those times and I heard quite a lot about the investigation into the Krays' affairs.

One of the notable points of that investigation was that it was not carried out at Scotland Yard but at the civilian headquarters, Tintagel House, on the Albert Embankment. The order to carry out this investigation in a secure environment and in utmost secrecy, with a team that was incorruptible and not likely to chatter about what was afoot, was allocated to Nipper Read. The reason that they had to be isolated was to prevent anyone of knowing what was going on; the greatest fear being that someone, other than the investigating team would hear something and for whatever reason pass it on. So being at Tintagel House with his personally selected team, Nipper Read carried out a very thorough and conclusive investigation. The gang was represented by a top barrister and I listened to the evidence being given, and I sensed by the way the questioning was going that a feeling of insecurity in the gang members had led to one of them protecting himself by letting some information be known to Nipper Read. Gradually this feeling of insecurity among the lower echelon of the Krays' gang meant they began talking, again to protect their own skins.

Two years before the state visit of Emperor Hirohito of Japan, his son the Crown Prince (now the emperor) came to England together with his wife. They stayed at Claridges Hotel and Stan Gammon and I escorted them. Nothing went wrong apart from the fact that we had to bring the Prince back from Oxford where he had made a visit without the Princess. The ride back, and bear in mind there were no motorways at that time, we managed within an hour, to which MacNabb commented, 'Nice ride Goodwin, a trifle fast I thought.'

This pre-emptive visit was I think to assess the mood of the general public with the Japanese Emperor coming some two years later. There were no great demonstrations and only on one occasion did two members of the Burma Star Association show their faces, holding up placards, showing that they were survivors of the Burma Campaign.

Brigadier Sir Geoffrey MacNabb, the government hospitality man was in attendance together with a Colonel Flower, who I think was learning the ropes. For this visit Her Majesty the Queen had supplied one of her Rolls Royce limousines for his use. Now these are very grand vehicles and are very high compared to a normal vehicle. Above the front seats situated in the centre line of the car was the post to carry, in normal circumstances the Royal Standard, but now it carried the Imperial Standard of the Emperor of Japan. This consisted of the royal chrysanthemum in gold wire.

Now comes the point to this whole story. At the Japanese Embassy on the Chelsea embankment a canopy had been erected over the front portico for the arrival of firstly, the Emperor, the host and secondly the Queen and Prince Philip, his guests.

The escort group led by Sergeant Jock Shields were in a basement room together with the Daimler hire chauffeurs and quite a few of them were moaning about the lack of refreshments. They always moaned so it was nothing new and in time you closed your mind to it. I was sitting there near the door when a servant of the embassy came in and asked, 'Mechanic?' No other word was said but I stood up and volunteered my services. I was taken across the passageway and shown into a room where another servant was holding the Imperial Standard complete with its mounting, which had broken as the car entered beneath the aforementioned canopy and had broken off. They had removed from the roof of the car the complete package which consisted of a black painted oak boss with mild steel and a bolt that affixed it to the car. On its upper end there was the Imperial Standard held onto a gold plated tube by an acorn shaped nut, also gold plated, with the whole lot fitted over a brass rod. This in fact had sheared off, hence the problem. I asked, mainly by sign language for a file which duly arrived. With the tang of the file I was fortunate enough to remove the broken end of the brass rod by gently unscrewing it. I then removed the Emperor's standard and handed it to the flunkies who were standing by the long end of the broken rod. I then gradually filed it down periodically offering it up to the threaded female part of the assembly until I considered there was sufficient brass rod in there to hold.

While I had been doing this the servants mentioned, 'Whiskey?' To which question I nodded my head. A single malt arrived and I indicated to the servant that they should fetch another policeman. One of them came in and enjoyed a drink and I asked that, quietly they should come in turn, which they did. On completion of the task many thanks were given and another bottle of scotch arrived which I secreted about my person.

On one occasion there was a slight cock up when Jock Shields pulled rank and insisted on going over the following day's route. His position when we set out over this route was in front of the car. The arrowhead ahead of him had no idea which route he had selected and it took us a few minutes to regain our composure. It was no good Jock going over a route without telling us, or better still without leading us on the journey.

As a Traffic Patrol one sometimes had to escort items through the streets of the metropolis to various destinations. From Charlton we would have to escort a ship's propeller from Stnes foundry. They were works of art and were carried flat on the back of a lorry. As they were large items we had to take a prescribed route to the docks on the north side of the Thames in the East End of London. Nearly all of these were done at night.

It was not the nicest of jobs if it was raining hard and was cold. Some items had to be escorted on mammoth multi-wheeled articulated II lorries to South Mimms on the A1 at the boundary with the next police force. What we always noticed and commented on was that it always felt that much colder once you went just a few miles further north. After leaving the load in the lay-by we would all adjourn to the ever-open transport cafe nearby and then a fast run back to the garage and home.

One job we had, and this was in a car, was to meet up with a Kent ambulance coming from that county with a serious spinal injury case on board. It was essential for the well-being of the patient that the ambulance had to maintain thirty miles per hour, no slowing down and certainly no speeding up, but just a constant speed. We drove in front of the ambulance with it close behind us so that at junctions where we had to go through the red light the motorists and other road users could see what was taking precedence over them. They were on route for the spinal unit at Stoke Mandeville.

On a lighter note we had to escort a large stainless steel vat about twelve feet in diameter from Woolwich to the Guinness Brewery at Park Royal to the west of London. There was no difficulty when the road was straight or reasonably so, it was when turning into another road that all our efforts were needed. It would have to swing out so far to get round the radius of the bends that we were almost stationary for quite a few minutes. At the brewery we were made very welcome with unlimited draught Guinness and the most finely cut chicken sandwiches. This particular job always took place on a Sunday morning when there was not so much traffic on the roads, and the route taken invariably followed the South Circular Road. After having taken our fill we then motored back to Lewisham.

The above are examples of police traffic patrols escorting items through the metropolis. We now come to the escorting of people of great importance. For this there was a Special Escort Group of class one motorcyclists.

There were various types of 'visit'. There was the state visit where the head of state, that is, a president or a monarch from abroad was the guest of the Queen. This would be when roads were closed off and a great deal of ceremony went into the exercise. The full escort group would then be used to give protection to the visitor as we formed a wall of motorcycles around the car containing the visitor and the retinue following on behind in other vehicles. There would be a single motorcyclist well ahead warning of our approach and another some distance behind letting the local constables know that the cavalcade had passed.

When Traffic Division, with the union of the old Traffic Garages and the Central Traffic Squad, the powers that be decided that for an escort involving say ten or eleven days two teams of two should be used doing alternate days. This happened when the Shah of Persia arrived to stay at Princes Gate. His wife arrived on a separate flight two hours later, when Ron Cross and I escorted her from the airport to the Persian Embassy at Princess Gate. When we arrived there, after getting out of her limousine, she came over to us, shook our hands and thanked us.

One journey we had to take was to the Borroughs Wellcome research laboratory at Cambridge. We were given the time that they were due to arrive there but they left the Embassy forty-five minutes late but we managed to make up thirty-five minutes on the journey and only arrived ten minutes late. After the visit there we then went to Wooten Hall where the Shah was to stay overnight as the guest of Lord Wooten. Ron Cross and I were to stay at the University Arms Hotel in Cambridge together with the Rolls Royce chauffeur and the Brigadier Sir Geoffrey McNabb, the government hospitality man and his second in command, Colonel Flower. At Wooten Hall we, that is the chauffeur, the local protection group from the Cambridgeshire Constabulary and the Special Branch man looking after the Shah were invited into the butler's pantry.

While in the butler's pantry we were fed very well indeed and Lady Wooten came in to enquire if everything was in order. Ron Cross leapt to his feet and made a right prat of himself by saying 'Yes, my lord,' to her ladyship. I heard the word cunt mentioned in very low terms from one of the local policeman. We were also visited by her maid, a great Austrian lady about thirty-ish who spent most of her conversation telling everybody that she was still a virgin. Later the team from the metropolis moved to take up residence in Cambridge and we were invited and gladly accepted a ride in the roller to the hotel. I had mentioned to Maria, the virgin, where I would be staying.

After a shower and changing into plain clothes Ron and I went to the restaurant, where McNabb and Flower had a job recognising us in mufti. Later that night while I was in bed the night porter informed me that there was a young lady in reception wanting to see me. It was Maria. Ten bob note to the porter and up she came to my room. I ushered her in, turned to close the door and when I faced into the room she was on the bed naked. I had to give her a ten shilling note for the taxi back to Wooten Hall. She gained access to the place through the open window in the butler's pantry where she aroused the local dog handler and his beast from their slumbers. It was years later that I met Lord Wooten's chauffeur at the House of Lords and he said that Maria still talked about me.

While at Princes Gate I was asked to escort the Shaharena to Harrods to do some shopping; it was to be just one Rolls Royce and me. I telephoned the station dealing with that place and asked the chief superintendent that the front of the shop be kept clear. I had first introduced myself and he laid on the necessary officers to keep the front clear. I arrived with the Rolls behind me, stopped, dismounted and stood talking to the local constable. I asked him that when we left would he please hold the traffic up while we did a u-turn. This he did and we arrived safely back at the

Embassy, I immediately rang the chief superintendent and thanked him for his help.

A dinner at the Mansion House, in the City of London, was put on by the Shah for business people and for the upper class Persians that were in London at that time. The event was opened by two trumpeters from the Household Cavalry and we had one close to us in full uniform who said that the biggest problem, when there were two of them to play a fanfare and that they were some distance and facing each other, was starting in unison. They managed however to get it right. We were sitting, that's the two of us, behind a thick curtain that ran all round the dining area which gave the servants passage way to the tables. One dropped off a bottle of champagne and we had to reach through the curtains to obtain two champagne flutes. We ate well and it was some time before a policeman came in and said that he'd left. We ran out to our bikes, pulling our helmet and other gear on and managed to catch them just as they turned onto the Albert Embankment. No harm was done and a good time was had by all. The rest of their visit went very well and they departed home, I should think, in good humour and well satisfied with their visit.

Time keeping was the essential ingredient of good escort duty: to get the VIP to his destination on time, not a minute before or a minute later. This was not always possible to achieve due to a late start of the journey, traffic hold ups or road works but we all set out to do our best and where there was a disruption to the well-timed journey we had to make up the time as best we could.

An example of this was when Chancellor Erhart of Germany was over and had a luncheon appointment with Her Majesty the Queen. On the official timetable he had to be at the Palace at twelve noon and we were allowed six minutes for the journey. Bearing in mind that the German Embassy was in Hanover Square, near St George's Hospital we would have to go to Hyde Park Corner turn down Constitutional Hill round the 'Wedding Cake' and into the Palace.

However he came out of the Embassy nine minutes before he was due at the Palace. I had with me four other members of the Escort Group and the golden rule was that where I went they followed. I would be out in front of the VIP's car with two members at its front wings and the other two keeping the back of the car clear. On my handlebars I had a clip holding an Ingersol pocket watch with large hands, wound up and dipped into polyurethane varnish to make it waterproof.

We set out from the Embassy, went round the Square and out at the bottom end and turned left to Grosvenor Gardens where we turned right, cut through to Buckingham Palace Road, down Birdcage Walk, left through Horse Guards and then left up The Mall. We entered the forecourt of Buckingham Palace just as Big Ben chimed midday.

Later, back at the Embassy I had the German diplomats apologise for the inconvenience they had caused and complimenting me on the action I had taken.

I would like to point out at this time Her Majesty will be in position at the Grand Entrance three minutes before her guest is due to arrive and will stay three minutes after. If one is early or if one is late the Queen has to be fetched and she would not be best pleased.

When John F Kennedy made a visit to Great Britain, Harold McMillan was the Prime Minister. We assembled at Heathrow, on a pleasant day, to escort the cavalcade to London.

A private individual had loaned a very nice open Bentley for the trip into town, so with the hood down and with the two leaders in the back, we set off. On leaving Heathrow Airport the nation's press photographers had spread themselves all over the road with their expensive cameras laying all over the roadway. I couldn't deviate and must confess that I had to ride over one or two of the more expensive items left out. Chalkie made sure that there was nothing to retrieve as he rolled over the rest of the debris. I wonder what they had to write on their insurance forms? I'm sure it would have made for a good read, and a good chuckle.

This was my first real escort. I had Chalkie White behind me and I was riding next to the front nearside wheel of the car. Now, as one couldn't know when the car was going to turn and by what degree, I had to spend most of the time looking at the Stars and Stripes that fluttered on the nearest wing. When it moved towards me I moved away, and with Chalkie calling out instructions the journey was made without incident.

When we arrived at Grosvenor Square, the home of the American Embassy, we knew we had a little time for a quick smoke so we secreted ourselves in the rear of the Embassy. We had only been there for a few minutes, not even enough to finish our cigarettes when a foot duty copper came over and told us that we were on the move again, so we threw down our smokes and took off like bandits, going the wrong way around the square, enabling us to quickly catch them up. This was known in those days as an FM start which roughly translated means fuck me they're going. Getting back we found that the President was being transferred from the open Bentley to a closed car because of our absence. Luckily we came just in the nick of time so that he could be reverted back into the Bentley.

We were always jumping on and off our bikes which is where we got the name, 'The Queen's Beasts,' or the 'Cocking the Leg Brigade'.

On another occasion I was also on patrol when Nixon came to town to visit the Queen at Buckingham Palace. One minute we were driving along in a very orderly fashion up The Mall and next we found ourselves caught off-guard when Nixon had decided to stop the car to shake hands with anyone that wanted to meet him. So we had to double back, regroup and make things look like nothing had happened. It was like taking a pram out and realizing that you've left the baby at home.

'Yes hello, I'm Dick! Nice to meet you too!'

During Tricky Dickey's same visit there was a banquet held at Buckingham Palace, and so after dropping him off we stomped about in the front courtyard of the august building, and spent our down time smoking, as most of us did in those days. We would also tell jokes, the filthier the better, and would never know when the event was going to finish and so had to stay there, killing all sorts of time. In the event that one had to spend a penny, there were facilities around to the side of the Palace. On one occasion I couldn't be bothered to take that walk and so just peed on the gravel between the parked limousines, kicking the gravel about to destroy all evidence. We longed to be back in our beds on those cold blustery nights, looking forward to the ridding of Her Majesty's guests.

One of the tasks I had to do on my own was to escort the Royal Plate of the Belgian Royal Family from Convoys Wharf, Deptford to the Belgian Embassy, in preparation for the Queen of the Belgians' state visit.

The plate was contained in a large wooden crate on the back of a flat top lorry. The job was easily done and it was to be a few days before I would see the contents of the box in all its finery. Two of us had the job of escorting the Queen during her visit, but this being the transitional period at the start of Traffic Division two other constables in a car were to follow on behind. I don't know who they were but they had no idea as to what the job entailed and had no sense of occasion. In fact it transpired in my view anyway that they were a miserable pair of bastards. An example of this was when our Queen and Prince Phillip were to attend a state banquet at the Belgian Embassy. The four of us were in a small room off the kitchen in the basement of the Embassy and watched through the glass door the Belgian Royal Chef preparing the meal. One of his staff was icing some of the three-tiered stands from the Royal Plate with such delicacy that when he had finished it hung down like lace from the top tier down to the bottom. Another man was preparing the vegetables and in fact carved the carrots so that they all looked the same and had the shape of barrels.

The chef was busy doing the more technical stuff and was sweating (the chef was in fact French) and we decided that the four of us should have a whip-round to buy the kitchen staff some beer. I went off down the road and at the local off-licence arranged for a crate of beer to be delivered to the Embassy. A man followed me back to the Embassy on his tradesman's bicycle and it was duly offered to the chef who thanked us and stated that we would eat what the Queen was going to have.

However this was some time away and the two who rode in the police car then started to moan, one of them stated that by staying where we were he would miss the Magic Roundabout on the television. One has to remember that we were going to eat a meal that we would never see the likes of again. They went on and on moaning and because of the atmosphere developing in the room, in front of the chef and kitchen staff I decided that we should leave. The two of us on the motorcycles made our way back to the garage at Lewisham and booked off. I believe the two in the car had come from Barnes Garage.

The following day I mentioned what had happened to Superintendent Fitzpatrick and he said that we should have stayed and ignored those in the car and that we should have let them leave if they wanted to. Apparently the powers that be chose not to have a car following on behind as it served no useful purpose and was a waste of manpower.

On another occasion I was in a car, in fact we had just received the Rover 3.5 with the automatic gearbox, with 202 TD Timber Woods known with great affection as the 'Talking Ring Spanner', when we were sent to Gallows Corner at the extreme north east boundary of the Metropolitan Police district to escort, and to guide an ambulance car containing a woman who was to be the first ever liver transplant, together with her surgeon to King's College Hospital, Denmark Hill in south London. I was driving and Timber gave great help as the operator in giving instructions to the ambulance to keep up with us and to keep Oscar Control at Scotland Yard informed as to our position minute by minute. At the Angel Islington and from then on we had foot duty controlling the traffic to help us through and we managed the journey in twenty minutes and were complimented on the drive by Oscar Control. At King's College Hospital the surgeon came over to us and described the drive as fantastic. His patient, a very attractive looking middle-aged woman also smiled at us and it is hard to believe that a fortnight after the transplant the poor lady died.

At another time I was delegated to escort Angus Ogilvy and Princess Alexander from Gatwick to Kensington Palace. My job was to protect the rear of their vehicle from the press which apparently, in South Africa where they had spent their honeymoon, had been absolute pests. At Gatwick Angus Ogilvy came over to me in the police car and asked whether or not his chauffeur could travel with us as he wished to drive his own car, a large Mark 119 Jaguar. I agreed to this and we followed him first to his flat in a side street off Park Lane and after a period of time to Kensington Palace. However once in Park Lane on the way to the Palace he stopped his car, got out and came over to me, saying that he could smell burning in his flat and could I discreetly do something about. I said that my job was to see the pair of them to Kensington Palace to which he replied that he knew his way there. Under the Ways and Means Act, as amended, I managed to get three fire officers in plain clothes transported in a police Hillman Minx to his flat where they discovered the smell to be coming from the electric motor in the fridge which was overheating. Mr Ogilvy had asked that no fuss be made about it, but wrongly I reported the incident on paper to West End Central Police Station where I asked that, at Angus Ogilvy's request, the matter shouldn't be passed to the Press Bureau. What happened? It was.

I was also faced with tasks in which I was solely engaged. A perfect example was when the Archbishop of Canterbury had to be at the House of Lords to vote during the Rhodesian problem. He was at the Fairfield Halls in Croydon and needed his journey to the House helped by an escort. This was no great problem and I eased his way to that august establishment. On our arrival there his chaplain, who accompanied him at all times, came over to me and thanked me on behalf of the Archbishop. Giving me a ten shilling note he said that the Archbishop, Doctor Ramsey, wanted me to have a drink on him, which I gladly did.

George Brown the Foreign Minister in the Wilson Cabinet was going to Wembley to watch England play Czechoslovakia in a football match. I had to get him there at six o'clock. We set out and bearing in mind that this was the evening rush hour, I had to carve up all the home bound commuters to get him there on time. When we arrived at Wembley the Empire Way that led up to the entrance was crowded with pedestrians and there was no way I could facilitate his progress through the throng of people. I made my own way through them and parked my bike near the main entrance to the stadium. The car arrived a few minutes later and George Brown alighted from his vehicle and shouted that this was not good enough. His body guard from Special Branch came over to me and I said to him in no uncertain terms that no way was I going to carve up the pedestrians as I had carved up the motorists getting him there and that he could get fucked and find his own way back. The Special Branch officer understood what had been entailed in the journey to Wembley. The remarks I made were, deliberately in the hearing of George Brown. What he had to understand was that to facilitate his progress others had to be inconvenienced.

I went into the Stadium where I was shown to a table that had been set for me for a meal before the match started. I had only just sat down among all the cutlery for the feast prepared when I was told that he was going. I got up, left the table and walked back towards the entrance to the arena. I passed George Brown sitting on steps with his head in his hands, pissed out of his mind. Near my motorcycle was a Rolls Royce with Richard Harris and two other actors, all dressed in sheepskin coats and was invited to have a wee dram with them, which I did and thoroughly enjoyed. We were chatting away when a young lady came up to me and asked if Daddy was about. It transpired that she was Miss Brown and when I told her that he was sitting on a staircase she asked whether he was drunk. I nodded and off she went with a big sigh. I was then approached by his bodyguard, the Special Branch man who asked that as a favour would I take them back to the official residence. I agreed to do so and so escorted them back. At the residence George Brown, alighting from his limousine, came over to me and apologised for the remarks he had made earlier. I said that there was no problem and we parted on satisfactory terms. I was cross with him, because, I had missed a delightful meal and had been unable to watch an international football match at Wembley. One bears no malice in these cases; it's the way of the world and it gives that lovely feeling, a most satisfying feeling, of being part of it.

WINSTON CHURCHILL

I escorted, together with Ron Cross, General De Gaulle from the French Embassy to St. Paul's Cathedral for the funeral of Winston Churchill. It was a sad day indeed and the end of an era in British history.

As a young lad I can remember his war time speeches on the radio, and the look of great confidence on my parents' faces. His speeches will always remain one of the finest examples of guiding confidence to the hard pressed British people.

He was quite right: in the end we were not defeated. After the war the general election opted for a Socialist government and Churchill slipped away into retirement. It was another sad day when that happened, and I think that in spite of what he had done during the war in leading us to victory, in essence he never recovered from that almost soviet inspired backlash.

After we had dropped De Gaulle off at St. Paul's we adjourned to a marquee in Green Park where we played cards, dealing them in time to the funeral march beat, and leaving the most moving feeling in the air while threading it's deathly passage to the cathedral. What was fascinating was that as Churchill was carried up river to his final resting place, the cranes at the side of the river dipped in salute as he passed. A sad day indeed and I know Winston is missed by many.

THE NEW RECRUITS

In the late Fifties a special traffic squad was set up to help with the increase in the volume of traffic in the centre of London. It was called the Central Traffic Squad.

The first contact I had with the a member of that new squad was at Marble Arch during the evening rush hour when one of its members dismounted from his motorcycle and ran into the traffic, coming to a halt by sliding on his ex -WD boots.

The feeling quite wrongly, was that they were the rejects of Traffic Patrol and hence were accepted for the Central Traffic Squad. I had been at the garage for quite some years before the whole of the traffic police were reorganized into Traffic Division, so we found ourselves rubbing shoulders with the members of the CTS.

As the Special Escort Group consisted of the motorcycle display team, all of whom were from Lewisham, and selected officers from the other garages, it caused some consternation when the powers that be decided to have the two specialist groups operate from Traffic Division M at Southwark.

Johnny Baldwin was to be in charge but all the lads at Lewisham refused to transfer from there with the exception of yours truly. I was asked to approach Ron Cross and see if I could get him to join our embryo team. His first reaction was, and I quote, 'Bollocks', but after a few days of gentle persuasion by me he did end up coming with us.

The Precision Team now consisted of two of the original team and we set about recruiting those we thought suitable and trained them ourselves. We practised at our usual place, Biggin Hill, where we would go through our moves for about twenty minutes and then rest for twenty to let the bikes cool down. During this time we would sunbathe and play volley ball with the ball that we kept in one of the drains at the end of the runway. It kept us fit and when we had an unexpected visit from Bill Fleming, I explained why the lads were playing about and not riding, and he accepted it.

In my early days with the team we would often pop into the pub at the corner of the airfield and have a pint whenever we needed topping up on a hot summer's day, leaving our bikes around the corner out of sight.

In the mornings we would meet at the Church Army canteen opposite the airfield where they did the best cheese and onion crispy rolls I have ever tasted.

Once we had all assembled we would then make our way to the practise area and get on with the job. What we aimed for was precision, hence the name of the team. We carried out all the moves in unison and in line. As the trainer I expected to see only one man when they were coming towards me in the line astern. In some moves, turns had to be made on the sound of the leader's horn. One would pause, and then turn. The whole thing went well on a good surface, smooth, good for both accelerating and braking, and was a delight to perform on. We all developed a sense of occasion. We were smartly turned out, riding bikes that gleamed and were mechanically in first class condition. All in all I like to think that in general we did a good public relations job for the Police Service and the Metropolitan Police in particular.

We would appear at many functions during the summer months and the atmosphere varied from place to place. We had some good days and some not so good days, but we all enjoyed our job. Some people would say that what we were doing was dangerous, and we would answer, that it was potentially so, but we were well trained and knew that our colleagues could be relied on.

THE TRUTH, THE WHOLE TRUTH, AND NOTHING BUT THE TRUTH.

I make no apology for the style or title I have given to people whom I have come into contact with in my years, nor do I apologize if I refer to the colour of their skin, nationality or of their religious beliefs. If I relate that I had to deal with a drunken Irishman then that is what took place.

I also realise that the correct term for homosexuals does not fall under the names that I have used, that is queers and poofs. That's just what we called them in those days and I still bring it forth with me today.

The End